Super Cheap Chicago Travel Guide

"I give you Chicago. It is not London and Harvard. It is not Paris and butter-milk. It is American in every chitling and sparerib. It is alive from snout to tail." —H. L. Mencken

Welcome to your guide to a Luxury Trip to Chicago on a budget!

This travel guide is your step-by-step manual for unlocking luxury hotels, enjoying the best culinary offerings and enjoying once-in-a-lifetime luxury experiences in Chicago at a fraction of the usual cost.

Everyone's budget is different, but luxury is typically defined by first or business class seats on the airplane, five-star hotels, chauffeurs, exclusive experiences, and delectable fine dining. Yes, all of these can be enjoyed on a budget.

Finding luxury deals in Chicago simply requires a bit of research and planning, which this book has done for you. This book is nearly 400 pages of bargains. We have packed this book with local insider tips and knowledge to save you at least £4,500, maybe even tens of thousands.

If the mere mention of the word luxury has you thinking things like "Money doesn't grow on trees," "I don't need anything fancy," "I don't deserve nice things," or "People who take luxury trips are shallow and materialistic/environmentally harmful/lack empathy, etc.," then stop. While we all know travel increases our happiness, research on the effects of luxury travel has proven even better results:

Reduced stress: A study published in the Journal of Travel Research found that individuals who visited luxury hotels reported feeling less stressed than those who in standard hotels.[1]

Increased happiness: A study conducted by the International Journal of Tourism Research found that luxury travel experiences lead to an increase in happiness and overall life satisfaction.[2] Researchers also found that luxury travel experiences can improve individuals' mental health by providing a sense of escape from daily stressors and enhancing feelings of relaxation and rejuvenation.

Enhanced creativity: Researchers found engaging in luxury travel experiences can stimulate creativity and lead to more innovative thinking.[3]

While all of this makes perfect sense; it feels much nicer to stay in a hotel room that's cleaned daily than in an Airbnb where you're cleaning up after yourself. What you might not know is that you can have all of that increased happiness and well-being without the expensive price tag.

[1] Wöber, K. W., & Fuchs, M. (2016). The effects of hotel attributes on perceived value and satisfaction. Journal of Travel Research, 55(3), 306-318.

[2] Ladhari, R., Souiden, N., & Dufour, B. (2017). Luxury hotel customers' satisfaction and loyalty: An empirical study. International Journal of Hospitality Management, 63, 1-10.

[3] Kim, S., Kim, S. Y., & Lee, H. R. (2019). Luxury travel, inspiration, and creativity: A qualitative investigation. Tourism Management, 71, 354-366.

The Magical Power of Bargains

Have you ever felt the rush of getting a bargain? And then found good fortune just keeps following you?

Let me give you an example. In 2009, I graduated into the worst global recession for generations. One unemployed day, I saw a suit I knew I could get a job in. The suit was £250. Money I didn't have. Imagine my shock when the next day I saw the exact same suit (in my size) in the window of a second-hand shop (thrift store) for £18! I bought the suit and after three months of interviewing, without a single call back, within a week of owning that £18 suit, I was hired on a salary far above my expectations. That's the powerful psychological effect of getting an incredible deal. It builds a sense of excitement and happiness that literally creates miracles.

I have no doubt that Chicago's picturesque 99999, ornate facades and rich history will uplift and inspire you but when you add the bargains from this book to your vacation, not only will you save a ton of money; you are guaranteed to enjoy a truly magical trip to Chicago.

Who this book is for and why anyone can enjoy budget travel

Did you know you can fly on a private jet for $500? Yes, a fully private jet. Complete with flutes of champagne and reclinable creamy leather seats. Your average billionaire spends $20,000 on the exact same flight. You can get it for $500 when you book private jet empty leg flights. This is just one of thousands of ways you can travel luxuriously on a budget. You see there is a big difference between being cheap and frugal.

When our brain hears the word "budget" it hears deprivation, suffering, agony, even depression. But budget travel need not be synonymous with hostels and pack lunches. You can enjoy an incredible and luxurious trip to Chicago on a budget, just like you can enjoy a private jet flight for 10% of the normal cost when you know how.

Over 20 years of travel has taught me I could have a 20 cent experience that will stir my soul more than a $100 one. Of course, sometimes the reverse is true, my point is, spending money on travel is the best investment you can make but it doesn't have to be at levels set by hotels and attractions with massive ad spends and influencers who are paid small fortunes to get you to buy into something you could have for a fraction of the cost.

This book is for those who love bargains and want to have the cold hard budget busting facts to hand (which is why we've included so many one page charts, which you can use as a quick reference), but otherwise, the book provides plenty of tips to help you shape your own Chicago experience.

We have designed these travel guides to give you a unique planning tool to experience an unforgettable trip without spending the ascribed tourist budget.

This guide focuses on Chicago's unbelievable bargains. Of course, there is little value in traveling to Chicago and not experiencing everything it has to offer. Where possible, we've included super cheap workarounds or listed the experience in the Loved but Costly section.

When it comes to luxury budget travel, it's all about what you know. You can have all the feels without most of the bills. A few days spent planning can save you thousands. Luckily, we've done the planning for you, so you can distill the information in minutes not days, leaving you to focus on what matters: immersing yourself in the sights, sounds and smells of Chicago, meeting awesome new people and feeling relaxed and happy.

This book reads like a good friend has travelled the length and breadth of Chicago and brought you back incredible insider tips.

So, grab a cup of tea or coffee, put your feet up and relax; you're about to enter the world of enjoying Chicago on the Super Cheap. Oh, and don't forget a biscuit. You need energy to plan a trip of a lifetime on a budget.

Discover Chicago

In the heart of the Midwest, where the wind sweeps off Lake Michigan and the skyline stands tall and proud, lies a city that has captured the imagination of travelers for generations. Chicago, known as the "Windy City," is a metropolis of architectural marvels, culinary delights, and a rich tapestry of history. While it may have a reputation for luxury and extravagance, this book is about a different kind of Chicago experience – one where you can savor all the city has to offer without breaking the bank. Welcome to "Super Cheap Chicago: A Luxury Trip on a Budget."

Chicago's history is as colorful as its skyline. It was here, at the beginning of the 19th century, that a small settlement emerged on the banks of the Chicago River. The city's strategic location as a transportation hub led to its rapid growth, transforming it into a bustling center of commerce. The Great Chicago Fire of 1871, a devastating event that burned much of the city to the ground, could not dampen the spirit of the Chicagoans. In fact, it was this very disaster that provided the city with an opportunity to rebuild, resulting in the birth of modern skyscrapers and the world-famous Chicago architectural style.

Speaking of architecture, Chicago boasts some of the most iconic and diverse structures in the world. From the historic elegance of the Chicago Water Tower to the cutting-edge designs of the Aqua Tower, the city is a living architectural museum. You can explore many of these buildings for free or at a fraction of the cost through guided tours or by simply wandering the streets and admiring their grandeur.
But Chicago is not just about buildings; it's also a city of neighborhoods, each with its own unique character. You can stroll through the artistic community of Wicker Park, enjoy the vibrant Latino culture of Pilsen, or savor authentic Chinese cuisine in Chinatown – all without emptying your wallet.

One of the best ways to experience Chicago's history and culture on a budget is through its world-class museums. Did you know that the Art Institute of Chicago offers free admission on certain days? You can admire masterpieces by Picasso, Grant Wood, and Georges Seurat without spending a dime. Additionally, the Chicago History Museum provides fascinating insights into the city's past, and many of its exhibitions can be enjoyed for free or at a low cost.

And what would a trip to Chicago be without indulging in its renowned culinary scene? While Chicago is famous for its deep-dish pizza and gourmet hot dogs, it's also home to a diverse array of international cuisines. From Mexican taquerias in the South Side to bustling ethnic markets in the North Side, you can savor authentic flavors without breaking your budget.

As we embark on this journey through Super Cheap Chicago, this guide will reveal the best-kept secrets, the hidden gems, and the budget-friendly alternatives that will help you experience the luxury side of Chicago without the hefty price tag. So fasten your seatbelt, sharpen your appetite, and get ready to explore the Windy City like a true insider. Welcome to the city where luxury and budget meet in perfect harmony – welcome to Super Cheap Chicago!

Some of Chicago's Best Bargains

Cheap Hotels near the Magnificent Mile

The Magnificent Mile, often referred to simply as "Mag Mile," is one of Chicago's most iconic and prestigious commercial districts. It stretches along a 13-block section of North Michigan Avenue in downtown Chicago, extending from the Chicago River to Oak Street. This historic and vibrant area has a rich history and is a great place to base yourself to explore the cities.

While nightly hotels rates average $300 you can find cheap deals on hotels near the magnificent mile on Groupon and priceline.com. Embassy Suites routinely offer $100 a night deals. They have free cook to order breakfast and free happy hour. You can also take the free trolley from there to the Magnificent Mile area.

Free entries!

Chicago offers many free and lesser-known activities and attractions for FREE. Here are some of the best:

- **Garfield Park Conservatory**: This beautiful botanical garden on Chicago's West Side is free to enter. Explore its lush greenhouses, filled with exotic plants and flowers.
- **National Museum of Mexican Art**: Located in the Pilsen neighborhood, this museum showcases a rich collection of Mexican art, and admission is free.
- **Smart Museum of Art**: Part of the University of Chicago, this museum offers free admission and features an impressive collection of art spanning different cultures and time periods.
- **Chicago Cultural Center**: This stunning building in the Loop hosts free exhibitions, performances, and events throughout the year. Don't miss the breathtaking Tiffany glass dome.
- **The 606**: This elevated park and trail system, often referred to as "Chicago's High Line," is perfect for walking, running, or biking. It's a great way to see the city from a unique perspective.
- **Loyola University Museum of Art (LUMA)**: LUMA offers free admission on Tuesdays and is home to a diverse collection of art and exhibitions.
- **Chicago Lakefront Trail**: Take a stroll or bike ride along the picturesque Lake Michigan shoreline. The views of the lake and skyline are magnificent, and the trail is free to use.
- **Baha'i House of Worship**: Located in nearby Wilmette, this architectural marvel is open to the public and offers a serene place for reflection.

Visit the Zoo for Free

The Lincoln Park Zoo is one of the last remaining free zoos in the country. You can explore a variety of animals and enjoy the beautiful park without spending a dime.

It is home to over one hundred animals, including elephants, zebras, and giraffes. In addition to its outdoor exhibits, the zoo also has indoor displays.

Attend Free Events

Neighborhood Festivals: Chicago hosts a variety of free neighborhood festivals throughout the year, such as the Chinatown Summer Fair, Square Roots Festival, Midsommarfest, and many more, celebrating the city's diverse culture, music, food, and community spirit.

Free Concerts: Check out free summer concerts at Millennium Park and other city parks. They often feature a wide range of musical genres and talented performers for FREE.

Chicago Public Libraries

Many libraries in Chicago offer free events and programs throughout the year. Some of the notable libraries that frequently host such events include:

- **Harold Washington Library Center:** The Harold Washington Library Center, the main library of the Chicago Public Library system, offers a robust calendar of free events, including author talks, lectures, workshops, and cultural programs.
- **Chicago Cultural Center:** Although not a library, the Chicago Cultural Center often hosts free events, including art exhibitions, music performances, and lectures, making it a cultural hub for the city.
- **Branch Libraries:** Chicago has numerous branch libraries throughout the city, and many of them host free events tailored to their local communities, such as reading clubs, children's storytimes, and educational workshops.
- **Sulzer Regional Library:** Located in the Lincoln Square neighborhood, Sulzer Regional Library is known for its diverse programming, including author visits, book clubs, and cultural events.

- **Harold Washington Library's YouMedia Center:** This special section within the Harold Washington Library Center caters to teenagers and offers free workshops, creative spaces, and events focused on technology, media, and art.
- **Woodson Regional Library:** Woodson Regional Library, located on the South Side, often hosts events related to African American history, culture, and literature.
- **Roden Branch Library:** Located in the Albany Park neighborhood, Roden Branch Library hosts a variety of free events, including language classes, book discussions, and arts and crafts activities.

Grab a Coupon Book

Go to the Navy Pier Guest Service Desk to get a coupon book. Inside this book are coupons for attractions, restaurants, and shops including the boat tours. And its totally FREE!

Visit Fashion Outlets of Chicago

The Fashion Outlets of Chicago is home to 130 designer stores, including Tory Burch, Gucci, and Bloomingdale's. The best part about Fashion Outlets of Chicago is that it's not difficult to get to. It's less than ten minutes from O'Hare International Airport, and is also easily accessible by public transportation. Whether you're flying in for a business trip or a weekend getaway, the mall makes it easy to arrive at your destination.

Download Shopping Apps

Download shopping apps like RetailMeNot, Shopular, or Coupon Sherpa to find additional coupons, deals, and discounts for stores at the Fashion Outlets

Oyster Happy Hours in Chicago

Several seafood spots in Chicago offer oyster happy hours. These deals are a great way to eat a variety of oysters while saving money.

- Lure Fishbar, During happy hours, you can enjoy a dozen oysters for $14, a half dozen Blue Points for $24, or a dozen fried oysters for $30.
- Lettuce Entertain - You can also enjoy oysters for $1 during their "spritz and shuck" happy hour. This happy hour is offered Wednesday through Friday from 4 p.m. to 7 p.m.
- The swanky River North supper club serves $1 oysters and Gulf shrimp during happy hour. They also offer half-priced cocktails, draft beer, and select wines during this time.

Eat like Royalty on the Cheap

The Lion Head in Lincoln Park They have a 10oz steak and potato for $7 on Mondays Sultans Market on North ave. $4 falafel and the best schwarma of your life.

Fat shallot food truck on Throop Street offers incredible truffel BLT's and truffle fries for under $8- http://thefatshallot.com/food-truck-menu/

How to Enjoy ALLO-CATING Money in Chicago

'Money's greatest intrinsic value—and this can't be overstated—is its ability to give you control over your time.' - Morgan Housel

Notice I have titled the chapter how to enjoy allocating money in Chicago. I'll use saving and allocating interchangeably in the book, but since most people associate saving to feel like a turtleneck, that's too tight, I've chosen to use wealth language. Rich people don't save. They allocate. What's the difference? Saving can feel like something you don't want or wish to do and allocating has your personal will attached to it.

And on that note, it would be helpful if you considered removing the following words and phrase from your vocabulary for planning and enjoying your Chicago trip:

- Wish

- Want

- Maybe someday

These words are part of poverty language. Language is a dominant source of creation. Use it to your advantage. You don't have to wish, want or say maybe someday to Chicago. You can enjoy the same things millionaires enjoy in Chicago without the huge spend.

'People don't like to be sold-but they love to buy.' - Jeffrey Gitomer.

Every good salesperson who understands the quote above places obstacles in the way of their clients' buying. Companies create waiting lists, restaurants pay people to queue outside in order to create demand. People reason if something is so in demand, it must be worth having but that's often just marketing. Take this sales maxim 'People don't like to be sold-but they love to buy and flip it on its head to allocate your money in Chicago on things YOU desire. You love to spend and hate to be sold. That means when something comes your way, it's not 'I can't afford it,' it's 'I don't want it' or maybe 'I don't want it right now'.

Saving money doesn't mean never buying a latte, never taking a taxi, never taking vacations (of course, you bought this book). Only you get to decide on how you spend and on what. Not an advice columnist who thinks you can buy a house if you never eat avocado toast again.

I love what Kate Northrup says about affording something: "If you really wanted it you would figure out a way to get it. If it were that VALUABLE to you, you would make it happen."

I believe if you master the art of allocating money to bargains, it can feel even better than spending it! Bold claim, I know. But here's the truth: Money gives you freedom and options. The more you keep in your account and or invested the more freedom and options you'll have. The principal reason you should save and allocate money is TO BE FREE! Remember, a trip's main purpose is relaxation, rest and enjoyment, aka to feel free.

When you talk to most people about saving money on vacation. They grimace. How awful they proclaim not to go wild on your vacation. If you can't get into a ton of debt enjoying your once-in-a-lifetime vacation, when can you?

When you spend money 'theres's a sudden rush of dopamine which vanishes once the transaction is complete. What happens in the brain when you save money? It increases feelings of security and peace. You don't need to stress life's uncertainties. And having a greater sense of peace can actually help you save more money.' Stressed out people make impulsive financial choices, calm people don't.'

The secret to enjoying saving money on vacation is very simple: never save money from a position of lack. Don't think 'I wish I could afford that'. Choose not to be marketed to. Choose not to consume at a price others set. Don't save money from the flawed premise you don't have enough. Don't waste your time living in the box that society has created, which says saving money on vacation means sacrifice. It doesn't.

Traveling to Chicago can be an expensive endeavor if you don't approach it with a plan, but you have this book which is packed with tips. The biggest other asset is your perspective.

How to feel RICH in Chicago

You don't need millions in your bank to **feel rich**. Feeling rich feels different to every person.

Here are things to see, do and taste in Chicago, that will have you overflowing with gratitude for your luxury trip to Chicago.

- Achieving a Michelin Star rating is the most coveted accolade for restaurants but those that obtain a Michelin Star are synonymous with high cost, but in Chicago there are restaurants with Michelin-stars offering lunch menus for 30 dollars or less!If you want to taste the finest seasonal local dishes while dining in pure luxury, visit the Most Affordable Michelin Restaurants in Chicago. Michelin's Bib Gourmand category includes restaurants that offer high-quality food at more affordable prices. Some of these restaurants are:
    - **Avec:** Avec is known for its Mediterranean-inspired small plates and communal dining. Prices vary, but you can enjoy a meal for around $30-$40 per person.
    - **Smalls Smoke Shack & More:** This BBQ joint offers affordable smoked meats and sides. Prices for a meal typically range from $10 to $20 per person.

- While money can't buy happiness, it can buy cake and isn't that sort of the same thing? Jokes aside, Sweet Mandy B's Bakery in Chicago have turned cakes and pastries into edible art. Visit to taste the most delicious croissant in Chicago.

- While you might not be staying in a penthouse, you can still enjoy the same views. Visit rooftop bars in Chicago, like Selva to enjoy incredible sunset views for the price of just one drink. And if you want to continue enjoying libations, head over to Mother's Ruin for a dirt-cheap happy hour, lots of reasonably priced (and delicious) cocktails and cheap delicious snacks.

- Walking out of a salon or barber shop with a fresh cut makes most people feel rich. As the maxim goes, if you look good, you feel good. If you crave that freshly blow-dried or trimmed look, become a hair model for https://www.salonapprentice.com. You'll receive a free or heavily discounted cut/colour or wash. Of course, always agree on the look with your stylist.

Those are just some ideas for you to know that visiting Chicago on a budget doesn't have to feel like sacrifice or constriction. Now let's get into the nuts and bolts of Chicago on the super cheap.

What you need to know before you visit Chicago

- Weather Variability: Chicago experiences four distinct seasons with significant weather fluctuations. Winters can be harsh with cold temperatures and snow, while summers can be hot and humid. Pack accordingly, depending on the season of your visit.
- Public Transportation: Chicago has an extensive public transportation system, including buses and the "L" train system. Consider purchasing a Ventra card for $5 or a CTA pass for convenient travel around the city.
- Chicago Neighborhoods: Chicago is known for its diverse neighborhoods, each with its own character and attractions. Explore areas like the Loop for downtown attractions, Wicker Park for hipster culture, and Chinatown for delicious cuisine.
- Museums and Cultural Institutions: Chicago is home to world-class museums such as the Art Institute of Chicago, the Field Museum, and the Museum of Science and Industry. Plan your visit to these attractions in advance and early in the day to make the most of your time.
- Food: Chicago is famous for its diverse culinary scene. Don't miss trying classic Chicago-style deep-dish pizza, Chicago-style hot dogs, and exploring the city's vibrant food trucks.
- Lakefront and Parks: Chicago boasts beautiful lakefront areas and parks. Take a stroll along Lake Michigan's shore, visit Millennium Park, and enjoy outdoor activities in Grant Park or Lincoln Park.

- Sports Enthusiasts: Chicago is a sports city with passionate fans. Depending on the season, consider catching a game at Wrigley Field (Chicago Cubs) or the United Center (Chicago Bulls and Chicago Blackhawks).
- Traffic and Parking: Traffic congestion and expensive parking can be common in the city. Consider using public transportation or rideshare services when possible to avoid the hassle of driving and parking.
- Architecture: Chicago is renowned for its architectural history. Taking an architectural boat tour is a must.

Planning your trip

When to visit

For convenient sightseeing weather May, June, September, and October are the best times to visit. Temperatures are usually mild during these months, with averages between 12°C and 21°C. May and June can be a little rainy, so pack an umbrella. Avoid the winter months, temperatures can drop to -25 degrees!

The seasons in Chicago and what to pack

Chicago experiences all four distinct seasons, each with its own weather patterns and temperatures. Here's an overview of the seasons and what to pack for each:
Spring (March to May):
* *Weather:* Spring in Chicago can be unpredictable, with gradually warming temperatures. It starts cool and gradually warms up.
  * What to Pack:
  * Layers: Light jackets, sweaters, and long-sleeve shirts for cooler days.
  * Comfortable walking shoes.
  * Umbrella, as spring showers are common.
  * Jeans or light pants.
  * Sunglasses and sunscreen as the sun becomes stronger.
Summer (June to August):
* *Weather:* Summers in Chicago are warm and humid, with occasional heatwaves.
  * What to Pack:

- Lightweight clothing, such as shorts, T-shirts, and sundresses.
- Sunscreen, sunglasses, and a hat for sun protection.
- Comfortable walking shoes or sandals.
- Swimsuit if you plan to visit the beach or pools.
- A reusable water bottle to stay hydrated.

Fall (September to November):
- *Weather:* Fall brings cooler temperatures and colorful foliage to the city.
  - What to Pack:
  - Sweaters, long-sleeve shirts, and a light jacket for cooler evenings.
  - Jeans or pants.
  - Comfortable walking shoes.
  - An umbrella and a light scarf.
  - Layers, as temperatures can vary during the day.

Winter (December to February):
- *Weather:* Winters in Chicago are cold, with snowfall and freezing temperatures.
  - What to Pack:
  - Heavy winter coat, insulated gloves, a hat, and a scarf.
  - Thermal layers, sweaters, and warm clothing.
  - Waterproof and insulated boots for snowy conditions.
  - Thick socks to keep your feet warm.
  - Hand and foot warmers if you plan to spend extended time outdoors.

Keep in mind that Chicago's weather can change quickly, so it's a good idea to check the forecast before your trip and be prepared for unexpected weather shifts, especially during transitional seasons like spring and fall. Layering is often a key strategy to adapt to changing conditions comfortably.

Visit Chicago on your birthday

Companies know rewarding customers on their birthdays will boost retention so many in Chicago go out of their way to surprise customers and make them feel special on their birthdays. Here are a list of American chains with birthday freebies and discounts: https://www.favoritecandle.com/free-birthday-meals/Chicago-Heights/IL

Visit Chicago on your birthday you can get well over $250 of free entries, meals, cakes and more. All you need is a valid ID to claim your birthday gifts.

Here are the free gifts:

- Free beauty gift from Sephora ($15)
- Free beauty gift from Ulta rewards
- Go to Build-a-Bear on a child's birthday and you pay your age for the bear! Great way to save $30 if you're travelling with kids.

Free food

- Fuddruckers: Get a special birthday main.
- Godiva: Join the Godiva Rewards Club and get an exclusive birthday gift.
- Great American Cookies: free cookie.
- Hard Rock Cafe: free dessert.
- Krispy Kreme - free dozen donuts
- Starbucks - free coffee

Weird and Wonderful Facts about Chicago

1. The Great Chicago Fire wasn't started by a cow: Contrary to popular belief, the 1871 Chicago Fire wasn't caused by Mrs. O'Leary's cow kicking over a lantern. The true cause remains a mystery.
2. The Twinkie was invented in Chicago: James Dewar created the iconic Twinkie snack cake in 1930 while working at the Continental Baking Company in Chicago.
3. Chicago River's color change: To celebrate St. Patrick's Day, the city has been dyeing the Chicago River green since 1962. It's a unique tradition that draws crowds each year.
4. The Ferris Wheel was invented in Chicago: The first Ferris Wheel was built by George Ferris for the 1893 World's Columbian Exposition in Chicago. It was a marvel of engineering at the time.
5. Chicago is home to the first ever skyscraper: The Home Insurance Building, completed in 1885, is often considered the world's first skyscraper. It stood at 10 stories tall, which was a groundbreaking achievement.
6. he Chicago "L": The Chicago "L" (short for "elevated") is one of the oldest and most extensive rapid transit systems in the world, dating back to 1892.
7. The Chicago "Bean": Officially known as "Cloud Gate," this iconic sculpture in Millennium Park is made of 168 stainless steel plates and reflects the city's skyline in a distorted way.
8. The Chicago Pedway: Chicago has a system of underground tunnels and overhead bridges known as the "Pedway" that helps pedestrians navigate the city during harsh weather. You can take a guided tour for free (more on that later).
9. The original Playboy Mansion: Hugh Hefner's first Playboy Mansion was in Chicago. The Playboy empire was launched from this city.

Accommodation

Your two biggest expenses when travelling to Chicago are accommodation and food. This section is intended to help you cut these costs dramatically without compromising on those luxury feels:

How to Book a Five-star Hotel consistently on the Cheap in Chicago

The cheapest four and five-star hotel deals are available when you 'blind book'. Blind booking is a type of discounted hotel booking where the guest doesn't know the name of the hotel until after they've booked and paid for the reservation. This allows hotels to offer lower prices without damaging their brand image or cannibalizing their full-price bookings.

Here are some of the best platforms for blind booking a hotel in Chicago:

1. Hotwire - This website offers discounted hotel rates for blind booking. You can choose the star rating, neighborhood, and amenities you want, but the actual hotel name will not be revealed until after you've booked.

2. Priceline - Once you've made the reservation, the hotel name and location will be revealed.
3. Secret Escapes - This website offers luxury hotel deals at discounted rates. You can choose the type of hotel you want and the general location, but the hotel name and exact location will be revealed after you book.
4. Lastminute.com - You can select the star rating and general location, but the hotel name and exact location will be revealed after booking. Using the Top Secret hotels you can find a four star hotel from $60 a night in Chicago - consistently! Most of the hotels featured are in the Grange Group. If in doubt, simply copy and paste the description into Google to find the name before booking.

Where to stay?

Families:

a. **The Loop:** Staying in the downtown area, specifically in the Loop, is a great option for families. It's close to major attractions like Millennium Park, the Art Institute of Chicago, and the Museum Campus (home to the Field Museum, Shedd Aquarium, and Adler Planetarium). There are many family-friendly hotels in this area.
b. **River North:** This trendy neighborhood has plenty of family-friendly hotels and is known for its vibrant restaurant scene and proximity to attractions like the Magnificent Mile and Navy Pier.
c. **Lincoln Park:** This residential neighborhood is a good choice for families looking for a quieter atmosphere. It's home to Lincoln Park Zoo and has many parks and playgrounds.
d. **Hotels with Suites:** Consider booking a suite-style hotel, which can provide more space for families. Some options include Embassy Suites, Homewood Suites, and Residence Inn by Marriott.

Budget:

a. **Hostels:** Chicago has several hostels that offer budget-friendly accommodation. The HI Chicago Hostel and Freehand Chicago are popular choices.
b. **Airbnb:** Renting a private room or entire apartment through Airbnb, which can often be more budget-friendly than traditional hotels. Look for options in neighborhoods like Logan Square, Wicker Park, or Uptown.
c. **Magnificent Mile:** While it's known for luxury shopping, you can also find budget-friendly hotels on or near the Magnificent Mile. Keep an eye out for deals and discounts.
d. **Chicago O'Hare Airport Area:** If you don't mind being a

bit further from downtown, you can find more affordable hotels near O'Hare International Airport. They often offer shuttle services to the airport and easy access to public transportation into the city.

e. **South Loop:** The South Loop area has some budget-
friendly hotels and is still relatively close to downtown attractions.

Chicago's Districts

Chicago is a diverse and vibrant city with a range of neighborhoods, each offering its own unique character, culture, and attractions. Here's a guide to some of the notable districts and neighborhoods in Chicago:

- The Loop:
    - The heart of Chicago's downtown, known for its iconic skyline, cultural institutions, and theaters.
    - Attractions: Millennium Park, Art Institute of Chicago, Chicago Symphony Orchestra, and Theater District.
    - Great for shopping along State Street and dining at renowned restaurants.
- River North:
    - An artsy and trendy neighborhood with a thriving nightlife scene.
    - Home to art galleries, boutiques, and some of the city's best restaurants.
    - The Riverwalk offers scenic views of the Chicago River.
- Magnificent Mile:
    - A high-end shopping district along Michigan Avenue, famous for luxury retailers and department stores.
    - Also home to historic landmarks like the Wrigley Building and the John Hancock Center.
- Streeterville:
    - Located near the lakefront, it's known for Navy Pier, Northwestern University's Chicago campus, and upscale living.
    - Navy Pier offers entertainment, dining, and boat tours.

- West Loop:
    - A foodie's paradise with a thriving culinary scene, including renowned restaurants and trendy bars.
    - The Fulton Market District is famous for its dining options.
- Lincoln Park:
    - A charming neighborhood with a mix of historic homes, parks, and tree-lined streets.
    - Lincoln Park itself features a zoo, conservatory, and lakefront beaches.
- Wicker Park and Bucktown:
    - Artsy and eclectic neighborhoods known for independent boutiques, galleries, and vibrant street art.
    - Great for nightlife with live music venues and craft cocktail bars.
- Lakeview:
    - Home to Wrigley Field, the historic baseball stadium.
    - Boasts a lively bar and restaurant scene in Wrigleyville.
    - The Lakeview neighborhood offers diverse dining options and vibrant LGBTQ+ nightlife in Boystown.
- Hyde Park:
    - Home to the University of Chicago and the Museum of Science and Industry.
    - Rich in cultural history and diverse dining options.
- Chinatown:
    - A cultural enclave with authentic Chinese restaurants, shops, and festivals.
    - Explore the Chinatown Gate and Ping Tom Memorial Park along the Chicago River.
- Pilsen:
    - Known for its Mexican heritage and vibrant arts scene.

- Murals and street art are prevalent, and the National Museum of Mexican Art is a highlight.
- Little Italy:
  - A historic neighborhood with Italian restaurants, bakeries, and the University of Illinois at Chicago.
  - Taylor Street is a food destination.
- Bronzeville:
  - A historic African-American neighborhood known for its rich cultural heritage.
  - Explore the Chicago Blues District and DuSable Museum of African American History.
- Rogers Park:
  - Located on the far north side and known for its diverse population.
  - Features beautiful lakefront parks and Loyola University Chicago.
- Andersonville:
  - A diverse and LGBTQ+-friendly neighborhood with a strong Swedish heritage.
  - Known for unique shops, restaurants, and the Andersonville Galleria.

Areas to exercise caution in Chicago

While Chicago is generally a safe city for tourists, like any major urban area, it has some neighborhoods with higher crime rates. It's essential to exercise caution and be aware of your surroundings when visiting certain areas. Here are some neighborhoods in Chicago where travelers are advised to exercise caution:

- **Englewood**: Englewood has a higher crime rate compared to other neighborhoods. It's best to avoid this area at night.

- **West Garfield Park**: This neighborhood has experienced higher crime rates in the past.
- **South Shore**: While South Shore has beautiful lakefront areas, it also has areas with elevated crime levels. Stay in well-traveled and well-lit areas if you visit.
- **West Englewood**: Similar to Englewood, West Englewood has a higher crime rate, and travelers should exercise caution in this neighborhood.
- **Fuller Park**: Fuller Park has been considered one of Chicago's more dangerous neighborhoods, and it's advisable to avoid it.
- **East and West Garfield Park**: These areas have seen higher crime rates, and it's recommended to exercise caution and avoid walking alone at night.
- **North Lawndale**: While parts of North Lawndale are improving, it still has some areas with elevated crime levels.
- **Roseland**: Roseland has experienced higher crime rates, and travelers should exercise caution when visiting.
- **Humboldt Park**: While Humboldt Park is home to a beautiful park, it has had higher crime rates in the past, so be cautious in certain areas, again especially true at night.

Suburbs to stay in Chicago that are cheap and safe

Oak Park: Located just west of Chicago, Oak Park is known for its historic architecture, tree-lined streets, and the former home of architect Frank Lloyd Wright. It offers a mix of affordable housing options and has a low crime rate. The area is well-served by public transportation, making it easy to access downtown Chicago.

Evanston: Situated to the north of Chicago along Lake Michigan, Evanston is home to Northwestern University. It has a diverse community, good schools, and a range of housing options. While it's relatively more expensive than some other suburbs, it's still more affordable than downtown Chicago and is considered safe.

Skokie: Located to the northwest of Chicago, Skokie is known for its strong sense of community and a variety of affordable housing options. It has a low crime rate and offers convenient access to public transportation.

Forest Park: This suburb is just west of Chicago and is known for its affordability. It's a short commute to the city, and the village has a welcoming atmosphere with parks and local businesses.

Berwyn: Berwyn is a budget-friendly suburb located just west of Chicago. It offers a range of housing options and has a relatively low cost of living compared to the city.

The town has a strong sense of community and is considered safe.

Cicero: Situated to the west of Chicago, Cicero is known for its affordable housing options and access to public transportation. While it has had challenges in the past, the safety situation has improved in recent years.

Niles: Located to the northwest of Chicago, Niles is a family-friendly suburb with affordable housing and good schools. It's a safe community and offers easy access to amenities.

Enjoy the Finest Five-star Hotels for a 10th of the Cost

Sleep cheap and enjoy five-star luxury during your waking hours. Many five-star hotels in Chicago offer day passes or access to their amenities like swimming pools, spa facilities, and fitness centers for non-guests. However, prices and availability can vary depending on the hotel and the time of year. Here are a few:

The Langham, Chicago:

Chuan Spa Day Pass: Prices start around $65 for access to the Chuan Spa, fitness center, and pool.
    Waldorf Astoria Chicago:

Four Seasons Hotel Chicago:

Spa Access Pass: Prices start at approximately $100 for access to the spa, fitness center, and pool. Spa treatments are extra.

The Peninsula Chicago:

Day Spa Pass: Prices start at around $150 and include access to the spa, fitness center, and pool. Spa services are additional.

Please note that these prices are approximate and can change over time. Additionally, availability may be limited, especially during peak seasons or busy weekends or when events such as weddings are taking place.

TOP TIP: AVOID The weekend price hike

Hotel prices skyrocket during weekends in peak season (June, July, August and December). If you can, get out of Chicago for the weekend you'll save thousands on luxury hotels. For example a room at a popular five-star hotel costs $180 a night during the week when blind-booking. That price goes to $500 a night for Saturday's and Sundays. Amazing nearby weekend trips are featured further on and planning those on the weekends could easily save you a ton of money and make your trip more comfortable by avoiding crowds.

Strategies to Book Five-Star Hotels for Two-Star Prices in Chicago

Use Time

There are two ways to use time. One is to book in advance. Three months will net you the best deal, especially if your visit coincides with an event. The other is to book on the day of your stay. This is a risky move, but if executed well, you can lay your head in a five-star hotel for a 2-star fee.

Before you travel to Chicago, check for big events using a simple google search 'What's on in Chicago', if you find no big events drawing travellers, risk showing up with no accommodation booked (If there are big events on demand exceeds supply and you should avoid using this strategy). If you don't want to risk showing up with no accommodation booked, book a cheap accommodation with free-cancellation.

Before I go into demand-based pricing, take a moment to think about your risk tolerance. By risk, I am not talking about personal safety. No amount of financial savings is worth risking that. What I am talking about is being inconvenienced. Do you deal well with last-minute changes? Can you roll with the punches or do you freak out if something changes? Everyone is different and knowing yourself is the best way to plan a great trip. If you are someone that likes to have everything pre-planned using demand-based pricing to get cheap accommodation will not work for you.

Demand-based pricing

Be they an Airbnb host or hotel manager; no one wants empty rooms. Most will do anything to make some revenue because they still have the same costs to cover whether the room is occupied or not. That's why you will find many hotels drastically slashing room rates for same-day bookings.

How to book five-star hotels for a two-star price

You will not be able to find these discounts when the demand exceeds the supply. So if you're visiting during the peak season, or during an event which has drawn many travellers again don't try this.

1. On the day of your stay, visit booking.com (which offers better discounts than Kayak and agoda.com). Hotel Tonight individually checks for any last-minute bookings, but they take a big chunk of the action, so the better deals come from booking.com.
2. The best results come from booking between 2 pm and 4 pm when the risk of losing any revenue with no occupancy is most pronounced, so algorithms supporting hotels slash prices. This is when you can find rates that are not within the "lowest publicly visible" rate.
3. To avoid losing customers to other websites, or cheapening the image of their hotel most will only offer the super cheap rates during a two hour window from 2 pm to 4 pm. Two guests will pay 10x difference in price but it's absolutely vital to the hotel that neither knows it.

Takeaway: To get the lowest price book on the day of stay between 2 pm and 4 pm and extend your search radius to include further afield hotels with good transport connections.

There are several luxury hotels outside of Chicago's city center that offer good transport connections to the city, as well as easy access to other nearby attractions. Here are a few options to consider:

- **Hyatt Regency O'Hare:** Located near O'Hare International Airport, the Hyatt Regency O'Hare offers luxury accommodations and easy access to the city via the Blue Line "L" train, which provides a direct route to downtown Chicago. The hotel also offers a complimentary shuttle to the airport.
- **The Westin O'Hare:** Another excellent airport hotel, The Westin O'Hare, provides comfortable rooms and easy access to downtown via the Blue Line "L" train. The hotel also offers shuttle service to O'Hare Airport.
- **The Langham, Chicago:** While technically in downtown Chicago, The Langham often offers competitive rates compared to other luxury hotels in the city center. It's located along the Chicago River and is within walking distance of attractions like Millennium Park and the Magnificent Mile.
- **Chicago Marriott Suites O'Hare:** This all-suite hotel is near O'Hare Airport and offers spacious accommodations. You can take advantage of the hotel's shuttle service to the airport and then use public transportation to reach downtown Chicago.
- **The Gwen, a Luxury Collection Hotel:** Located in the Magnificent Mile area, The Gwen offers luxury accommodations and is often more affordable than some of the city's top downtown hotels. It's well-situated for exploring downtown Chicago and is close to the Red Line "L" train for easy transit.
- **Renaissance Chicago North Shore Hotel:** Situated in Northbrook, a northern suburb of Chicago, this hotel provides a comfortable stay with access to downtown

via the Metra train. It's a good choice if you prefer a quieter, suburban setting.

- **The Westin Lombard Yorktown Center:** Located in Lombard, a western suburb, this hotel offers luxury accommodations and is conveniently located near the Lombard Metra station, providing a straightforward way to reach downtown Chicago.
- **The Herrington Inn & Spa (Geneva, IL):** If you're open to staying outside the immediate Chicago area, this boutique hotel in Geneva, Illinois, offers a luxurious escape along the Fox River. You can take the Metra train from Geneva to Union Station in downtown Chicago.

These are just a few examples of luxury hotels outside of Chicago's city center with good transport connections to the city and opportunities for last-minute discounts.

Priceline Hack to get a Luxury Hotel on the Cheap

Priceline.com has been around since 1997 and is an incredible site for sourcing luxury Hotels on the cheap in Chicago.

Priceline have a database of the lowest price a hotel will accept for a particular time and date. That amount changes depending on two factors:

1. Demand: More demand high prices.
2. Likelihood of lost revenue: if the room is still available at 3pm the same-day prices will plummet.

Obviously they don't want you to know the lowest price as they make more commission the higher the price you pay.

They offer two good deals to entice you to book with them in Chicago. And the good news is neither require last-minute booking (though the price will decrease the closer to the date you book).

'Firstly, 'price-breakers'. You blind book from a choice of three highly rated hotels which they name. Pricebreakers, travelers are shown three similar, highly-rated hotels, listed under a single low price.' After you book they reveal the name of the hotel.

Secondly, the 'express deals'. These are the last minute deals. You'll be able to see the name of the hotel before you book.

To find the right luxury hotel for you at a cheap price you should plug in the neighbourhoods you want to stay in, an acceptable rating (4 or 5 stars), and filter by the amenities you want.

You can also get an addition discount for your Chicago hotel by booking on their dedicated app.

How to trick travel Algorithms to get the lowest hotel price

Do not believe anyone who says changing your IP address to get cheaper hotels or flights does NOT work. If you don't believe us, download a Tor Network and search for flights and hotels to one destination using your current IP and then the tor network (a tor browser hides your IP address from algorithms. It is commonly used by hackers). You will receive different prices.

The price you see is a decision made by an algorithm that adjusts prices using data points such as past bookings, remaining capacity, average demand and the probability of selling the room or flight later at a higher price. If knows you've searched for the area before ip the prices high. To circumvent this, you can either use a different IP address from a cafe or airport or data from an international sim. I use a sim from Three, which provides free data in many countries around the world. When you search from a new IP address, most of the time, and particularly near booking you will get a lower price. Sometimes if your sim comes from a 'rich' country, say the UK or USA, you will see higher rates as the algorithm has learnt people from these countries pay more. The solution is to book from a local wifi connection - but a different one from the one you originally searched from.

Best Price Performance Hotels in Chicago with Frequent Last-minute Discounts

Motel 6: Motel 6 is known for its budget-friendly accommodations and can be found in various neighborhoods around Chicago.

Super 8: Super 8 offers affordable options in and around the city, particularly near O'Hare International Airport.

Red Roof Inn: Red Roof Inn has several locations in the Chicago area, and they often provide competitive rates for budget-conscious travelers.

Extended Stay America: This chain specializes in extended-stay accommodations, but they also offer nightly rates and can be cost-effective for longer stays.

Days Inn: Days Inn can offer affordable rates in various parts of the city, so it's worth checking for deals.

Howard Johnson: Howard Johnson provides budget-friendly options, especially near O'Hare Airport.

Rodeway Inn: You can find Rodeway Inn locations in the Chicago area with competitive pricing.

Universities renting dorm rooms in summer in Chicago

Many universities in Chicago offer dorm room accommodations to tourists during the summer months when students are on break. These accommodations can provide a private room for super cheap during summer when prices are crazy. Here are some options.

University of Chicago:

The University of Chicago offers summer housing in various residence halls. Prices can range from $40 to $100+ per night, depending on the type of room and amenities.

Northwestern University - Evanston Campus:

Northwestern University, located in nearby Evanston, offers summer housing options. Prices typically vary but can be competitive compared to hotels in downtown Chicago.

DePaul University:

DePaul University may offer summer housing options at their Lincoln Park and Loop campuses. Prices can vary based on location and room type.

Loyola University Chicago:
Loyola University Chicago has offered summer housing at its Lake Shore Campus in the past, with prices that can be budget-friendly compared to downtown hotels.

University Center - Chicago:

The University Center, located in downtown Chicago, houses students from multiple universities. It may offer summer accommodations to tourists at competitive rates.

Columbia College Chicago:

Columbia College Chicago may provide dorm room rentals during the summer months. Prices can vary depending on the type of room and location.

Stay in a Retreat Centre

Staying in a convent or monastery near Chicago can provide a unique and peaceful lodging experience and cost from $60 a night:

Franciscan Retreats and Spirituality Center (Dittmer, Missouri):

While not in Chicago, the Franciscan Retreats and Spirituality Center in nearby Dittmer, Missouri, offers a peaceful retreat experience. They have modest accommodations, and the cost can vary based on the type of room and the length of your stay. It's best to contact them directly for current pricing and availability.

Sisters of Mercy Convent (Aurora, Illinois):
The Sisters of Mercy Convent in Aurora, Illinois, has been known to offer accommodations for retreats and overnight stays.

How to get last-minute discounts on owner rented properties

In addition to Airbnb, you can also find owner rented rooms and apartments on www.vrbo.com or HomeAway or a host of others.

Nearly all owners renting accommodation will happily give renters a "last-minute" discount to avoid the space sitting empty, not earning a dime.

Go to Airbnb or another platform and put in today's date. Once you've found something you like start the negotiating by asking for a 25% reduction. A sample message to an Airbnb host might read:

Dear HOST NAME,

I love your apartment. It looks perfect for me. Unfortunately, I'm on a very tight budget. I hope you won't be offended, but I wanted to ask if you would be amenable to offering me a 25% discount for tonight, tomorrow and the following day? I see that you aren't booked. I can assure you, I will leave your place exactly the way I found it. I will put bed linen in the washer and ensure everything is clean for the next guest. I would be delighted to bring you a bottle of wine to thank you for any discount that you could offer.

If this sounds okay, please send me a custom offer, and I will book straight away.

YOUR NAME.

In my experience, a polite, genuine message like this, that proposes reciprocity will be successful 80% of the time.

Don't ask for more than 25% off, this person still has to pay the bills and will probably say no as your stay will cost them more in bills than they make. Plus starting higher, can offend the owner and do you want to stay somewhere, where you have offended the host?

In Practice

To use either of these methods, you must travel light. Less stuff means greater mobility, everything is faster and you don't have to check-in or store luggage. If you have a lot of luggage, you're going to have fewer of these opportunities to save on accommodation. Plus travelling light benefits the planet - you're buying, consuming, and transporting less stuff.

Hotels.com Loyalty Program

This is currently the best hotel loyalty program with hotels in Chicago. The basic premise is you collect 10 nights and get 1 free. hotels.com price match, so if booking.com has a cheaper price you can get hotel.com, to match. If you intend to travel more than ten nights in a year, its a great choice to get the 11th free.

Don't let time use you.

Rigidity will cost you money. You pay the price you're willing to pay, not the amount it requires a hotel to deliver. Therefore if you're in town for a big event, saving money on accommodation is nearly impossible so in such cases book three months ahead.

How to trick travel Algorithms to get the lowest hotel price

Do not believe anyone who says changing your IP address to get cheaper hotels or flights does NOT work. If you don't believe us, download a Tor Network and search for flights and hotels to one destination using your current IP and then the tor network (a tor browser hides your IP address from algorithms. It is commonly used by hackers). You will receive different prices.

The price you see is a decision made by an algorithm that adjusts prices using data points such as past bookings, remaining capacity, average demand and the probability of selling the room or flight later at a higher price. If knows you've searched for the area before ip the prices high. To circumvent this, you can either use a different IP address from a cafe or airport or data from an international sim. I use a sim from Three, which provides free data in many countries around the world. When you search from a new IP address, most of the time, and particularly near booking you will get a lower price. Sometimes if your sim comes from a 'rich' country, say the UK or USA, you will see higher rates as the algorithm has learnt people from these countries pay more. The solution is to book from a local wifi connection - but a different one from the one you originally searched from.

How to save money on food in Chicago

Use 'Too Good To Go'

Chicago offers plenty of food bargains; if you know where to look. Thankfully the app 'Too Good to Go' is turning visitors into locals by showing them exactly where to find the tastiest deals and simultaneously rescue food that would otherwise be wasted. In Chicago you can pick up a $15 buy of baked goods, groceries, breakfast, brunch, lunch or dinner boxes for $2.99. You'll find lots of fish and meat dishes on offer in Chicago, which would normally be expensive.

How it works? You pay for a magic bag (essentially a bag of what the restaurant or bakery has leftover) on the app and simply pick it up from the bakery or restaurant during the time they've selected. You can find extremely cheap breakfast, lunch, dinner and even groceries this way. Simply download the app and press 'my current location' to find the deals near you in Chicago. .What's not to love about relicious food thats a quarter of the normal price and helping to drive down food waste?

An oft-quoted parable is 'There is no such thing as cheap food. Either you pay at the cash registry or the doctor's office'. This dismisses the fact that good nutrition is a choice; we all make every-time we eat. Cheap eats are not confined to hotdogs and kebabs. The great thing about using Too Good To Go is you can eat nutritious food cheaply: fruits, vegetables, fish and nut dishes are a fraction of their supermarket cost.

Japan has the longest life expectancy in the world. A national study by the Japanese Ministry of Internal Affairs and Communications revealed that between January and May 2019, a household of two spent on average ¥65,994 a month, that's $10 per person per day on food. You truly don't need to spend a lot to eat nutritious food. That's a marketing gimmick hawkers of overpriced muesli bars want you to believe.

Check out this local Facebook group (https://www.facebook.com/groups/415004949343308/) where people share pictures of the food they picked up from restaurants and supermarkets in Chicago. It's a great way to see what's on offer and find food you'll love.

Breakfast
If you stay somewhere with a free breakfast, eat smart. Don't eat sugary cereals or white flour rich pastries if you don't want to be hungry an hour later. Before leaving your hotel or checking out, find some fresh fruit, water, and granola in the fitness centre or coffee in the lobby or business centre. If your hotel doesn't have free breakfast, don't take it. You can always eat cheaper outside. Sunrise Cafe has the best cheap breakfast we found. Here you can pick up pancakes for less than $4.

Visit supermarkets at discount times.
You can get a 50 per cent discount around 5 pm at the Whole Foods supermarkets on fresh produce. The cheaper the supermarket, the less discounts you will find, so check Whole Foods and at 5 pm. Some items are also marked down due to sell-by date after the lunchtime rush so its also worth to check in around 3 pm.

Use delivery services on the cheap.

Take advantage of local offers on food delivery services. Most platforms including Door Dash offer $10 off the first order in Chicago.

Here are some more tips to help you dine on a budget:

Discount Dining Apps: Use dining apps like Groupon, Yelp, or local Chicago deals apps to find discounts and special offers at restaurants.

Explore Neighborhoods: Venture beyond downtown to neighborhoods like Pilsen, Logan Square, and Chinatown, where you can find delicious and affordable meals at local eateries.

Food Trucks and Stands: Look for food trucks and street food vendors for budget-friendly, tasty options. Chicago has a diverse food truck scene.

Lunch Specials: Many restaurants in Chicago offer lunch specials, which are often more affordable than dinner menus. Take advantage of these deals.

Happy Hour: Enjoy discounted drinks and appetizers during happy hour at bars and restaurants. This can be an excellent way to try out upscale places at a lower cost.

Chicago-Style Hot Dogs and Pizza: Opt for Chicago's famous hot dogs or deep-dish pizza, which tend to be more filling and reasonably priced compared to fine dining.

Dine-In Deals: Some restaurants offer discounts for dining in during off-peak hours. Check if your chosen restaurant has any early bird or late-night specials.

BYOB Restaurants: Look for restaurants that allow you to bring your own bottle of wine or beer. This can save you money on alcohol.

Food Challenges: Some restaurants offer food challenges where you can eat a large meal for free (or at a reduced cost) if you finish it within a certain time frame.

Here are a few restaurants in Chicago known for their food challenges:

- **The Wiener's Circle:** This iconic Chicago hot dog stand is known for its "Superdawg Challenge." It involves eating a giant Superdawg with all the fixings and a large order of cheese fries in under five minutes.
- **Fatso's Last Stand:** Fatso's offers a "Belly Buster Challenge" that requires participants to eat a massive 5-pound burger with all the toppings and a large order of fries within a certain time frame.
- **Paddy Long's:** Paddy Long's is famous for its "Bacon Bomb Challenge." Participants must eat a massive 5-pound bacon-wrapped meatloaf along with sides in a set amount of time.
- **Jake Melnick's Corner Tap:** Known for its spicy food challenges, Jake Melnick's offers the "XXX Wings Challenge" where participants must eat a dozen extremely spicy wings within a certain time limit.
- **Cafe El Tapatio:** Cafe El Tapatio in Chicago's Andersonville neighborhood has a "Taco Challenge" where participants attempt to eat 10 tacos in 30 minutes. Winners receive a t-shirt and bragging rights.
- **Quaker Steak & Lube:** Located in nearby Edison, Indiana, Quaker Steak & Lube offers the "Triple Atomic Challenge" involving incredibly spicy chicken wings. Participants must sign a waiver before attempting.

Cheapest supermarkets

Chicago has several supermarket chains and stores where you can find affordable groceries. Prices can vary depending on your location within the city and the specific items you're purchasing. Here are some of the well-known and generally budget-friendly supermarket options in Chicago:

- **Aldi**: Aldi is known for its low prices and store-brand products. They have multiple locations throughout Chicago.
- **Save-A-Lot**: Save-A-Lot is a discount grocery store chain with various locations in Chicago offering lower-priced groceries.
- **Pete's Fresh Market**: Pete's Fresh Market is a locally-owned grocery chain that often offers competitive prices, especially on fresh produce and international foods.
- **Tony's Fresh Market**: Tony's is another local grocery chain known for its competitive prices, fresh produce, and a variety of products.
- **Food 4 Less**: Food 4 Less is a discount supermarket with multiple locations in the Chicago area, offering a wide range of groceries at lower prices.
- **Mariano's**: While Mariano's is not typically known as a discount store, they do offer competitive pricing on many products, and they have various locations throughout the city.
- **Walmart Supercenters**: Walmart Supercenters can be found in and around Chicago, offering a range of groceries at competitive prices.
- **Shop & Save Market**: Shop & Save Market is a local chain with a focus on affordability and value.

- **Cermak Fresh Market**: Cermak Fresh Market is a locally-owned supermarket chain with competitive prices and a diverse selection of products.
- **Jewel-Osco**: While Jewel-Osco is a larger supermarket chain, they often have weekly sales and promotions that can help you save on groceries.

20 Cheap Eats

Chicago is known for its diverse food scene, and you can find delicious cheap eats across the city. Here are 20 must-try affordable dishes and tips on what to eat:

1. **Chicago-Style Hot Dog**: Try a classic Chicago-style hot dog topped with yellow mustard, chopped onions, sweet pickle relish, tomato wedges, a dill pickle spear, sport peppers, and celery salt. Skip the ketchup!
2. **Italian Beef Sandwich**: Savor an Italian beef sandwich with thinly sliced roast beef, giardiniera, and au jus. Get it dipped for extra flavor.
3. **Deep-Dish Slice**: Grab a slice of deep-dish pizza from a pizzeria like Art of Pizza or My Pi Pizza. It's a filling and iconic Chicago dish.
4. **Jibarito**: Try a jibarito, a Puerto Rican sandwich made with fried green plantains instead of bread, filled with your choice of meat, cheese, and toppings.
5. **Tamale**: Sample a tamale, a Mexican dish of masa dough filled with seasoned meat, cheese, or vegetables, often served with salsa.
6. **Gyros**: Enjoy a gyro sandwich with seasoned meat (typically lamb or beef), lettuce, tomatoes, onions, and tzatziki sauce, wrapped in pita bread.
7. **Chicago-Style Popcorn**: Get a mix of caramel and cheese popcorn, a local favorite. Garrett Popcorn Shops is a popular spot for this snack.
8. **Maxwell Street Polish Sausage**: Sink your teeth into a Maxwell Street Polish sausage, a grilled Polish sausage on a bun with grilled onions and mustard.
9. **Tacos**: Head to a local taqueria for affordable and tasty tacos. Try different fillings like al pastor, carne asada, and carnitas.

10. **Korean Tacos**: Check out food trucks or Korean restaurants for Korean tacos, which blend Korean flavors with Mexican tortillas.
11. **Soul Food**: Try soul food dishes like fried chicken, macaroni and cheese, and collard greens at local soul food restaurants or food festivals.
12. **Tamale Guy**: Look out for the "Tamale Guy," who sells tamales late at night in various bars around the city.
13. **Pizza by the Slice**: Visit local pizzerias for New York-style pizza slices with various toppings.
14. **Mexican Paletas**: Cool down with Mexican paletas (popsicles) in a variety of flavors, including fruit, cream, and even chili.
15. **Banh Mi Sandwich**: Taste a Vietnamese banh mi sandwich with a variety of fillings, including grilled pork or tofu, pickled vegetables, and fresh herbs.
16. **Pierogies**: Try pierogies, dumplings filled with ingredients like potatoes, cheese, and meat. They're often served with sour cream.
17. **Hot Doug's-Style Hot Dogs**: Visit "The Wiener's Circle" for a unique Chicago experience and try their signature char-dog or chocolate shake.
18. **Cuban Sandwich**: Sample a Cuban sandwich with roasted pork, ham, Swiss cheese, pickles, and mustard on Cuban bread.
19. **Elote**: Savor elote, Mexican street corn typically slathered with mayonnaise, cheese, chili powder, and lime juice.
20. **Doughnuts**: Indulge in doughnuts from local bakeries like Do-Rite Donuts or Stan's Donuts. Try classic flavors or unique creations.

DIY Budget Food Tour

Here's a budget-friendly food tour itinerary to taste some of the best flavors in Chicago without breaking the bank. This tour covers a variety of cuisines and neighborhoods, offering a diverse culinary experience.

Stop 1: Maxwell Street Market (South Loop)
- Start your day at the Maxwell Street Market, a historic market with a wide range of affordable street food vendors. Try a Maxwell Street Polish sausage with grilled onions and mustard. Don't forget to explore the market for other snacks and treats.

Stop 2: Pilsen Neighborhood (Mexican Cuisine)
- Head to Pilsen, a vibrant neighborhood known for its Mexican cuisine. Visit a local taqueria for delicious tacos with options like al pastor, carne asada, or carnitas. Wash it down with a refreshing horchata.

Stop 3: Chinatown (Chinese Cuisine)
- Next, make your way to Chinatown. Stop by a Chinese bakery like Chiu Quon Bakery for affordable buns and pastries. Try a char siu bao (barbecue pork bun) or a custard tart.

Stop 4: Greektown (Greek Cuisine)
- Drive to Greektown and enjoy a gyro sandwich with seasoned meat, lettuce, tomatoes, onions, and tzatziki sauce wrapped in pita bread. You can find budget-friendly options at places like Artopolis Bakery.

Stop 5: Little India (Indian Cuisine)
- Explore Chicago's Little India in the West Rogers Park neighborhood. Visit a restaurant like Ghareeb Nawaz for a flavorful and affordable Indian meal. Try their biryani or a vegetarian thali.

Stop 6: Bakeries (Dessert)

- Treat yourself to some dessert at one of Chicago's bakeries. Stan's Donuts or Do-Rite Donuts offer a variety of doughnuts, including classics and unique flavors.

Stop 7: Local Ice Cream Shop

- Wrap up your budget food tour with a visit to a local ice cream shop like Original Rainbow Cone. Enjoy their iconic five-flavor ice cream cone or a scoop of your favorite flavor.

Additional Tips:

- Consider sharing dishes with a friend to try more items without overeating or overspending.
- Check for daily specials, happy hour deals, or combo meals to save money at various stops.
- Use public transportation or rideshares to get around the city efficiently.
- Bring cash for some vendors that may not accept credit cards.

First day in Chicago for under $30

Experiencing your first day in Chicago for under $30 is more than possible!

Morning (Under $5):
- Grab Breakfast (Under $5):
  - Start your day with a budget-friendly breakfast at a local bakery or café. You can get a pastry or breakfast sandwich with coffee for under $5.
- Explore Millennium Park (Free):
  - Head to Millennium Park, one of Chicago's iconic attractions. Take a selfie at "The Bean" (Cloud Gate) and stroll through the beautiful gardens.

Midday (Under $10):
- Art Institute of Chicago (Free for Illinois Residents, Otherwise Under $10):
  - Visit the Art Institute of Chicago during their free hours for Illinois residents (typically on certain weekdays). If you're not an Illinois resident, admission is under $10 for students and residents of neighboring states.
- Lunch in the Loop (Under $10):
  - Enjoy a budget-friendly lunch in the Loop area. Consider a food truck, food court, or a fast-food restaurant with affordable options.

Afternoon (Under $10):
- Chicago Riverwalk (Free):

- Take a walk along the Chicago Riverwalk, where you can enjoy the scenic views of the river, architecture, and public art installations.
- Chicago Cultural Center (Free):
  - Visit the Chicago Cultural Center, which hosts free art exhibitions and cultural events. It's a beautiful historic building to explore.

Evening (Under $5):
- Dinner (Under $5):
  - Opt for a budget-friendly dinner at a local eatery, such as a hot dog stand or a slice of pizza. You can find classic Chicago food for under $5.
- Navy Pier (Free Admission, Some Attractions Extra):
  - Head to Navy Pier in the evening to enjoy the stunning views of Lake Michigan and the city skyline. While some attractions may have admission fees, simply strolling along the pier is free and beautiful.

Total Estimated Cost: Under $30

Unique bargains I love in Chicago

Chicago has some truly unique bargains you won't find elsewhere:

Thrifting: Chicago has a thriving thrift store scene, making it a fantastic place to find unique clothing, accessories, and home decor items at affordable prices. Check out thrift shops like Village Discount Outlet, Unique Thrift Store, and Goodwill for hidden treasures.

Chinatown: Chicago's Chinatown is a great place to shop for unique Asian products, including ceramics, home decor, and traditional teas.

Discount Bookstores: If you're a book lover, Chicago has several discount and used bookstores where you can find great reads at bargain prices. Myopic Books in Wicker Park is a favorite among book enthusiasts.

How to Find Super Cheap Flights to Chicago

At the time of writing British Airways are flying to Chicago direct for around $289 return.

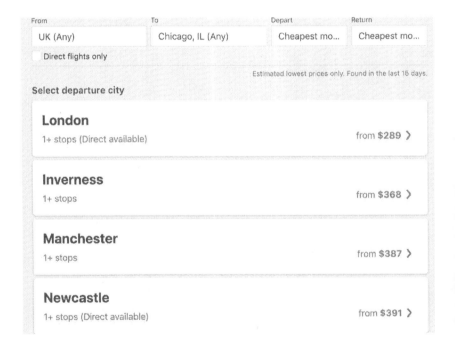

Luck is just an illusion. Anyone can find incredible flight deals. If you can be flexible you can save huge amounts of money. In fact, the biggest tip I can give you for finding incredible flight deals is simple: find a flexible job. Don't despair if you can't do that theres still a lot you can do. The following pages detail the exact method I use to consistently find cheap flights to Chicago.

Book your flight to Chicago on a Tuesday or Wednesday

Tuesdays and Wednesdays are the cheapest days of the week to fly. You can take a flight to Chicago on a Tuesday or Wednesday for less than half the price you'd pay on a Thursday Friday, Saturday, Sunday or Monday.

Start with Google Flights
I conduct upwards of 50 flight searches a day for readers. I use google flights first when looking for flights. I put specific departure but broad destination (e.g Europe) and usually find amazing deals.

The great thing about Google Flights is you can search by class. You can pick a specific destination and it will tell you which time is cheapest in which class. Or you can put in dates and you can see which area is cheapest to travel to.

But be aware Google flights does not show the cheapest prices among the flight search engines but it does offer several advantages

1. You can see the cheapest dates for the next 8 weeks. Other search engines will blackout over 70% of the prices.
2. You can put in multiple airports to fly from. Just use a common to separate in the from input.
3. If you're flexible on where you're going Google flights can show you the cheapest destinations.
4. You can set-up price tracking, where Google will email you when prices rise or decline.

Once you have established the cheapest dates to fly go over to skyscanner.net and put those dates in. You will find sky scanner offers the cheapest flights.

Get Alerts when Prices to Chicago are Lowest

Google also has a nice feature which allows you to set up an alert to email you when prices to your destination are at their lowest. So if you don't have fixed dates this feature can save you a fortune.

Baggage add-ons

It may be cheaper and more convenient to send your luggage separately with a service like sendmybag.com Often the luggage sending fee is cheaper than what the airlines charge to check baggage. Visit Lugless.com or luggage-free.com in addition to sendmybag.com for a quotation.

Loading times

Anyone who has attempted to find a cheap flight will know the pain of excruciating long loading times. If you encounter this issue use google flights to find the cheapest dates and then go to skyscanner.net for the lowest price.

Always try to book direct with the airline

Once you have found the cheapest flight go direct to the airlines booking page. This is advantageous in the current covid cancellation climate, because if you need to change your flights or arrange a refund, its much easier to do so, than via a third party booking agent.

That said, sometimes the third party bookers offer cheaper deals than the airline, so you need to make the decision based on how likely you think it is that disruption will impede you making those flights.

More flight tricks and tips

www.secretflying.com/usa-deals offers a range of deals from the USA and other countries. For example you can pick-up a round trip flight non-stop from from the east coast to johannesburg for $350 return on this site

Scott's cheap flights, you can select your home airport and get emails on deals but you pay for an annual subscription. A free workaround is to download Hopper and set search alerts for trips/price drops.

Premium service of Scott's cheap flights.
They sometime have discounted business and first class but in my experience they are few and far between.

JGOOT.com has 5 times as many choices as Scott's cheap flights.

kiwi.com allows you to be able to do radius searches so you can find cheaper flights to general areas.

Finding Error Fares
Travel Pirates (www.travelpirates.com) is a gold-mine for finding error deals. Subscribe to their newsletter. I recently found a reader an airfare from Montreal-Brazil for a $200 round trip (mistake fare!). Of course these error fares are always certain dates, but if you can be flexible you can save a lot of money.

Things you can do that might reduce the fare to Chicago:--
• Use a VPN (if the booker knows you booked one-way, the return fare will go up)
• Buy your ticket in a different currency

If all else fails...

If you can't find a cheap flight for your dates I can find one for you. I do not charge for this nor do I send affiliate links. I'll send you a screenshot of the best options I find as airlines attach cookies to flight links. To use this free service please review this guide and send me a screenshot of your review - with your flight hacking request. I aim to reply to you within 12 hours. If it's an urgent request mark the email URGENT in the subject line and I will endeavour to reply ASAP.
philgtang@gmail.com

How to Find CHEAP FIRST-CLASS Flights to Chicago

Upgrade at the airport

Airlines are extremely reluctant to advertise price drops in first or business class tickets so the best way to secure them is actually at the airport when airlines have no choice but to decrease prices dramatically because otherwise they lose money. Ask about upgrading to business or first-class when you check-in. If you check-in online look around the airport for your airlines branded bidding system. For example KLM at Amsterdam have terminals where you can bid on upgrades.

Use Air-miles

When it comes to accruing air-miles for American citizens **Chase Sapphire Reserve card** ranks top. If you put everything on there and pay it off immediately you will end up getting free flights all the time, aside from taxes.

Get 2-3 chase cards with sign up bonuses, you'll have 200k points in no time and can book with points on multiple airlines when transferring your points to them.

Please note, this is only applicable to those living in the USA. In the Bonus Section we have detailed the best air-mile credit cards for those living in the UK, Canada, Germany, Austria, Spain and Australia.

How many miles does it take to fly first class?
First class from Chicago to Bangkok (one way) costs 180,000 miles.

Arriving

There are two international airports in Chicago: O'Hare International Airport and Chicago Midway Airport. You can use public transit to reach the city from both nearby airports both are $5. From O'Hare (the airport most travellers arrive to) the Blue Line 'L' train will take you from O'Hare to downtown in about 45 minutes for $5.00.

O'Hare is the larger of the two airports and is located about 18 miles (29 kilometers) northwest of downtown Chicago.

To get from O'Hare to the city cheaply here are all the options.

CTA "L" Train: The Chicago Transit Authority (CTA) offers the Blue Line "L" train service from O'Hare to downtown. It's an affordable option, and the fare is typically under $5.
Airport Shuttle Services: Shared airport shuttle services like Go Airport Express and Airport Express provide cost-effective transportation to various parts of the city.
Uber/Lyft: Ride-sharing services like Uber and Lyft are available and often offer competitive rates compared to taxis.
Midway International Airport (MDW):
Midway is located about 10 miles (16 kilometers) southwest of downtown Chicago.

To get from Midway to the city cheaply:

CTA "L" Train: The CTA Orange Line "L" train runs directly from Midway to downtown Chicago. The fare is typically under $3.

Airport Shuttle Services: Shared airport shuttle services and bus services are available from Midway to downtown Chicago.

If you plan to use public transportation frequently during your stay, consider purchasing a multi-day CTA pass for unlimited rides on buses and trains.

Check for any airport shuttle deals or discounts offered by your hotel or accommodations.

Consider the timing of your flight arrival or departure. Late-night or early-morning flights may limit your transportation options, so plan accordingly.

Need a place to store luggage?
Use stasher.com to find a convenient place to store your luggage cheaply. It provides much cheaper options than airport and train station lockers in Chicago.

Getting Around

Getting around Chicago cheaply can be easy with a combination of public transportation, walking, and budget-friendly transportation options. Here are some cost-effective ways to navigate the city:

- Chicago Transit Authority (CTA):
    - The CTA operates buses and trains (known as the "L") throughout the city.
    - **Ventra Card**: Purchase a Ventra Card to pay for fares on CTA buses and trains. It offers discounts compared to single-ride tickets.
    - **Unlimited Ride Passes**: Consider purchasing a 1-day, 3-day, or 7-day unlimited ride pass for unlimited use of CTA buses and trains during the specified period. These passes offer great value for tourists.

- Walking:
    - Chicago is a pedestrian-friendly city with many attractions, restaurants, and shops with-

in walking distance of each other. Explore neighborhoods on foot to save money and discover hidden gem

Divvy Bikes:

- Divvy Bikes is Chicago's official bike-sharing system, with numerous docking stations throughout the city.
- Single Ride: $4.95 for a 30-minute ride.
- Explorer Pass: $15 for unlimited 3-hour rides within a 24-hour period.
- Annual Membership: Prices vary, with unlimited 45-minute rides included in the membership.

Lime (Scooters and Bikes):

- Lime offers both electric scooters and traditional pedal bikes for rent.
- Scooter Unlock Fee: Typically around $1, plus a per-minute rate (e.g., $0.39 per minute).
- Bike Unlock Fee: Around $1 for traditional pedal bikes, plus a per-minute rate.
- Lime also offers various promotions, discounts, and monthly passes.

Bird (Scooters):

- Bird provides electric scooters for rent in Chicago.
- Scooter Unlock Fee: Typically around $1, plus a per-minute rate (e.g., $0.39 per minute).
- Bird also occasionally offers promotions and discounts for riders.

Spin (Scooters):

- Spin offers electric scooters for rent in the city.
- Scooter Unlock Fee: Usually around $1, with a per-minute rate (e.g., $0.39 per minute).
- Spin may offer special pricing for daily or monthly passes.

JUMP (Bikes and Scooters by Uber):

- JUMP offers both electric scooters and pedal-assist bikes in Chicago.
- Scooter Unlock Fee: Around $1, plus a per-minute rate.
- Ride-Sharing Services:

- Uber and Lyft operate in Chicago and are often more affordable than taxis. Use their apps to request rides to specific destinations. ALWAYS Google for promo codes. They offer $50 free credit to new users. All you need is an email and credit card not associated with an account.
- Metra Commuter Rail:
    - If you plan to explore areas outside the city center, consider using the Metra commuter rail system. Fares are distance-based, and they offer weekend passes for unlimited rides on Saturdays and Sundays.
- Airport Transportation:
    - Use the CTA "L" train to travel to and from O'Hare and Midway airports. It's a cost-effective option.
    - Shared airport shuttle services and buses are also budget-friendly options.
- Trolley and Free Shuttles:
    - Some neighborhoods and attractions offer free trolley or shuttle services during specific times or seasons. **Navy Pier Trolley:** Navy Pier operates a free trolley service that runs seasonally and connects Navy Pier to popular destinations in the downtown area, including Millennium Park, the Magnificent Mile, and more.

Discount Passes

Chicago offers several discount passes that provide access to multiple attractions at a reduced price.

The key to making any of these worth the price tag is to squeeze a lot in on one day. If you can see 3 - 4 attractions a day you can save 55%.

- Chicago CityPASS:
    - Price: $108 for adults, $89 for children (ages 3-11).
        - Includes admission to five top Chicago attractions:
        - Shedd Aquarium
        - Skydeck Chicago
        - Field Museum
        - Museum of Science and Industry OR 360 Chicago Observation Deck
        - Art Institute of Chicago OR Chicago History Museum
        -
- Chicago Explorer Pass:
    - Price: Varies based on the number of attractions chosen (3, 4, 5, or 7 attractions).
    - Choose from a list of over 25 attractions, including museums, cruises, and tours.
    - Prices start at around $69 for 3 attractions.
    - If you plan to visit a lot of paid attractions in Chicago, such as Skydeck, 360 Chicago, the Aquarium and Field Museum you can save money starting early and doing them all in a day with the pass if you can fit in 6 attractions (average $40 entrance fee) you can save 55% on the entry fees.

- Go Chicago Card:
  - Price: Varies based on the number of days (1, 2, 3, 4, 5, or 7 days) and attractions chosen.
  - Offers access to over 25 attractions, tours, and activities.
  - Prices start at around $79 for a 1-day pass.
- Chicago South Shore Cultural Center Membership:
  - Price: $40 per year for an individual or $75 for a family.
  - Provides access to the South Shore Cultural Center, which includes a golf course, beach, and cultural programs.

An alternative to all high paid attractions is the library at the University of Chicago. Take the escalators up to the Winter Garden at Harold Washington Library to visit the stunning architecture free of charge.

The library at the University of Chicago.

London House has a FREE STUNNING rooftop view from its hotel.

Top Attractions

Here are the top attractions in Chicago, along with money-saving tips for each:

- Art Institute of Chicago:
    - Money-Saving Tip: Visit on Thursday evenings when admission is free for Illinois residents.
- Millennium Park:
    - Money-Saving Tip: Enjoy free outdoor concerts, art installations, and events held in the park throughout the year.
- Shedd Aquarium:
    - Money-Saving Tip: Purchase a CityPASS or Go Chicago Card for discounted admission to Shedd Aquarium and other top attractions.
- Skydeck Chicago (Willis Tower):
    - Money-Saving Tip: Buy tickets online in advance to skip the lines and potentially save on admission.
- Field Museum:
    - Money-Saving Tip: Illinois residents can enjoy free admission on select dates. Check the museum's website for details.
- Navy Pier:
    - Money-Saving Tip: Look for special deals on Navy Pier's website and the coupon book at the service desk for discounts on rides and attractions.
- Museum of Science and Industry:
    - Money-Saving Tip: Consider visiting during free museum days for Illinois residents or check for discounts with CityPASS or other passes.
- 360 Chicago Observation Deck:

- Money-Saving Tip: Purchase tickets online to save on admission and avoid waiting in line.
- The Chicago Theatre:
  - Money-Saving Tip: Look for discounted tickets or special offers for theater shows and concerts. More on that later.
- Chicago River Architecture Tours:
  - Money-Saving Tip: Opt for a daytime tour, which tends to be more affordable than evening cruises. Book on Groupon for the best prices.
- Chicago Botanic Garden:
  - Money-Saving Tip: Admission is free, but there's a parking fee. Consider taking public transportation or biking to save on parking.

Start with this Free Tour

Forget exploring Chicago by wandering around aimlessly. Start with a free organised tour. Nothing compares to local advice, especially when travelling on a budget. Ask for their recommendations for the best cheap eats, the best bargains, the best markets, the best place for a particular street eat. Perhaps some of it will be repeated from this guide, but it can't hurt to ask, especially if you have specific needs or questions. At the end you should leave an appropriate tip (usually around $5), but nobody bats an eye lid if you are unable or unwilling to do so, tell them you will leave a good review and always give them a little gift from home - I always carry small Vienna fridge magnets (because thats where I live) and I always tip the $5, but it is totally up to you.

Chicago Greeter Program:

The Chicago Greeter Program offers free guided tours by local volunteers who are passionate about their city. Visitors can request a personalized tour based on their interests and explore various neighborhoods and cultural highlights. Website: Chicago Greeter Program. **Book in advance to avoid disappointment!**

INSIDER CULTURAL INSIGHT

In the 1920's infamous Al Capone controlled Chicago. In an era when the government wasn't helping the poor, Capone set up soup kitchens positioning himself successfully as a folk hero and winning support from locals to continue his criminal enterprise.

INSIDER MONEY SAVING TIP

The Chicago Loop tour is a two-hour walk that takes you inside the Loop district, exploring the interiors of some of the city's most iconic buildings. You will learn about the history of Chicago and get an inside look at some of its most iconic architecture. The tour is also free and takes you through less touristy areas of the city. You can also join a tour of Millennium Park for a fun and relaxing experience. https://freetoursbyfoot.com/free-chicago-loop-tour/

Helicopter Tour

Helicopter tours in Chicago can be quite expensive due to the unique and exhilarating experience they offer. Seeing the architecture from the air is just mind-blowing. You may find some cost-effective options. Here's a general idea of the cheapest helicopter tour in Chicago:

Tour Operator: Vertiport Chicago
- **Tour**: Vertiport Chicago Helicopter Tour (8-10 minutes)
- **Price**: $159 per person

Architectural Cruise

Chicago Architectural Foundation is the organization that runs the cruises of Chicago's architecture. Stop by the CAF Shop and Tour Center at 224 S. Michigan Avenue to see a fantastic free exhibition about Chicago's skyline.

The Navy Pier (where the cruises depart) reaches half a mile into Lake Michigan. Walk out and you have spectacular views of the city. The Navy Pier is also home to the Ferris Wheel, Chicago Children's Museum, Chicago Shakespeare Theater, the Crystal Gardens, an IMAX Theater and more.

Wrap up warm if you're going to do a cruise. It's much colder than you would expect out on Lake Michigan. Check for cruise deals on Groupon, you can often pick one up for $10.

INSIDER MONEY SAVING TIP

If you visit during 17-18 October you can do free tours of more than 200 architectural masterpieces as part of Open House Chicago (www.openhousechicago.org).

Incredible views

Rooftop bars in Chicago offer great views of the city, but they can be expensive. Here are some rooftop bars that are known for having more budget-friendly options:

- Cindy's Rooftop:
    - Located at the Chicago Athletic Association Hotel, Cindy's Rooftop offers stunning views of Millennium Park and Lake Michigan. While some cocktails can be pricey, they often have happy hour specials with drinks priced around $10-12.
- The J. Parker:
    - The J. Parker is atop the Hotel Lincoln in Lincoln Park and offers fantastic views of the city and Lake Michigan. They have a happy hour menu with drinks starting at around $8.
- Drumbar:
    - Drumbar is located on the rooftop of the Raffaello Hotel and has a stylish, speakeasy vibe. They offer a happy hour menu with select cocktails priced at around $10.
- ZED451 Rooftop Lounge:
    - ZED451 has a rooftop lounge with a relaxed atmosphere. They often have happy hour specials with drinks starting at around $8-10.
- Fremont Rooftop Bar:
    - Located in River North, Fremont offers a rooftop bar with a lively atmosphere. They have daily drink specials, and some cocktails can be found for around $10.
- Apogee Lounge:
    - Apogee Lounge is known for its creative cocktails and stylish rooftop setting. While some drinks can be pricier, they may have

happy hour specials with select cocktails for around $10-12.

Do a Beer Tasting

Chicago has a vibrant craft beer scene, and you can find reasonably priced beer tastings at various breweries and bars. Prices for beer tastings can vary depending on the brewery and the type of tasting experience you choose. Here are a few options for affordable beer tastings in Chicago:

- Revolution Brewing Company:
    - Revolution Brewing offers reasonably priced brewery tours that often include a tasting session. Prices may start at around $10-15, which typically includes a flight of their beers.
- Half Acre Beer Company:
    - Half Acre offers brewery tours with tastings, and the prices can be quite reasonable, starting at around $10-15. They also have a taproom where you can sample their beers.
- Lagunitas Brewing Company:
    - Lagunitas offers free tours of their Chicago brewery, and while the tour itself is free, they often have reasonably priced tasting options available.
- Forbidden Root Brewery:
    - Forbidden Root offers brewery tours and tastings at an affordable price, starting at around $10-15, which includes a flight of their unique brews.
- Sketchbook Brewing Co.:
    - Located in nearby Evanston, Sketchbook Brewing Co. offers affordable tasting flights, with prices typically ranging from $10-15.

Be in a TV audience

Chicago offers opportunities to be part of live studio audiences. Some TV shows use audience ticketing websites to distribute tickets. Websites like 1iota (1iota.com) and On-Camera Audiences (ocatv.com) are popular platforms where you can search for TV show tapings in Chicago and FREE request tickets.

Score Discounted Theater Tickets

Check out the Hot Tix booth or TodayTix app for discounted theater tickets to see top-notch productions in Chicago.

Theatre has a rich history in Chicago, dating back to the mid-19th century. Over the years, the city has become a major hub for both commercial and experimental theater.

Getting Discounted Theatre Tickets in Chicago:
- **Hot Tix:** Hot Tix is a service provided by the League of Chicago Theatres that offers discounted tickets for same-day and next-day performances. You can visit their booth at the Chicago Cultural Center or check their website for listings and prices.
- **Student and Senior Discounts:** Many theaters in Chicago offer discounted tickets to students and seniors. Be sure to check with the specific theater and bring valid ID.

- **Rush Tickets:** Some theaters release rush tickets a few hours before a performance at a reduced price. These tickets are often available for purchase at the box office and are first-come, first-served.
- **Digital Lotteries:** Some productions offer digital lotteries through mobile apps or websites, where you can enter for a chance to purchase discounted tickets to popular shows.
- **Preview Performances:** Preview performances of shows are often less expensive than regular performances and can offer a chance to see a production before it officially opens.

If your under 30 you might want to consider the The Steppenwolf RED card. he Steppenwolf RED card is a good option, since it gives you seventy-eight percent off of any show, and includes discounts on in-theatre drink prices.

There are other options to save on tickets, such as the Goodman Theatre's Half-Price Mezzanine tickets. This option is available online at 10am daily, and allows you to purchase tickets at half price. You can also purchase discounted tickets at the Chicago Loop Theatre District, a cluster of theaters in the city's Loop neighborhood.

Chicago Theatre Week is an annual event that features a variety of value-priced tickets, and is presented by the League of Chicago Theatres. The event is held every year from March 3-5, and features more than 100 performances.

Northwestern University is one of the USA'S top-rated university theater programs. Tickets are much cheaper than the prices downtown - around $10 - $30. The campus is in Evanston, 12 miles north of the Loop.

Church Hop

Chicago is home to numerous historic and architecturally significant churches, each with its own unique history and features. Here are some of the best churches in Chicago, along with notable aspects to look out for inside each church:

Holy Name Cathedral:

- **History:** This Roman Catholic cathedral was built in the late 1800s and has been a symbol of the city's Catholic heritage.
- **Highlights:** Admire the stunning Gothic architecture, intricate stained glass windows, and the impressive pipe organ.

Fourth Presbyterian Church:
- **History:** Built in 1914, this church is a prominent example of Gothic Revival architecture.
- **Highlights:** Explore the beautiful interior with intricate stone carvings, stained glass, and a tranquil courtyard garden.

Rockefeller Memorial Chapel (University of Chicago):
- **History:** This neo-Gothic chapel was dedicated in 1928 as a gift from John D. Rockefeller.
- **Highlights:** Marvel at the intricate stone detailing, stunning stained glass windows, and the soaring vaulted ceiling.

St. James Chapel (Quigley Seminary):
- **History:** Built in 1917, this chapel is known for its Beaux-Arts architecture.
- **Highlights:** Admire the ornate marble and decorative artwork, including the impressive high altar.

First United Methodist Church:
- **History:** Completed in 1924, this church is a blend of Gothic and Romanesque styles.
- **Highlights:** Don't miss the beautiful stained glass windows, the Skinner organ, and the peaceful courtyard garden.

St. Michael's Church (Old Town):
- **History:** This historic Catholic church dates back to 1852 and is known for its stunning architecture.

- **Highlights:** Explore the interior with its ornate altar, intricate stained glass, and historic murals.

St. Hedwig's Church:
- **History:** Established in 1888, St. Hedwig's is a Polish Catholic church in the heart of Chicago's Polish community.
- **Highlights:** Look for the striking stained glass windows, decorative altar, and Polish heritage displays.

St. Paul's United Church of Christ:
- **History:** Founded in 1883, this church features a unique blend of Gothic and Romanesque elements.
- **Highlights:** Explore the stunning sanctuary, with its intricate woodwork, stained glass, and historic organ.

Attend Free public lectures in Chicago

Chicago is a city with a rich cultural and educational scene, and you can often find free public lectures and talks on a wide range of topics. Here are some places and resources where you can discover free public lectures in Chicago:

- Universities and Colleges:
    - Many universities in Chicago, such as the University of Chicago, Northwestern University, and DePaul University, host free public lectures and talks by professors, researchers, and guest speakers. Check their event calendars for upcoming lectures.
- Museums:
    - Museums like the Art Institute of Chicago, Museum of Science and Industry, and Chicago History Museum frequently organize free lectures, panel discussions, and gallery talks related to their exhibits.
- Cultural Centers:
    - The Chicago Cultural Center, located in the historic building, hosts a variety of free events, including lectures, exhibitions, and performances.
- Think Tanks and Research Institutes:
    - Chicago is home to various research institutions and think tanks that often organize free lectures on topics ranging from policy and economics to science and technology. Examples include the Chicago Council on Global Affairs and the Illinois Policy Institute.
- Public Events and Festivals:

- Keep an eye out for free lectures and discussions as part of public events and festivals in Chicago, such as the Chicago Humanities Festival and Printers Row Lit Fest.
- Libraries and Bookstores:
  - Some libraries and bookstores, such as the Seminary Co-op Bookstore and Women & Children First, host author readings and book talks that are free to attend.

Do More Free Tours

The Chicago Cultural Center offers a free tour at 1pm Monday to Friday in its 1897 Beaux-Arts building with vaulted lobby, mosaics and 2 stained-glass domes. This was the best tour we did in Chicago, the guides are retirees who are extremely knowledgable about Chicago's history.

Address: 78 E. Washington St.

- **Chicago Architecture Center:** While the Chicago Architecture Center offers paid tours, they also occasionally host free walking tours and programs. Check their website or visit their location for information on any upcoming free tours.
  Website: Chicago Architecture Center

Miller Brewing Company offers free tours: visit the packaging plant, where 2000 cans are filled each minute and indulge in a

generous free beer tasting session.
<u>Address:</u> 4251 W State St

The Gold Coast is one of Chicago's richest neighbourhoods. On Wednesdays you can do a free tour of the Charnley-Persky House. See what home were built before the skyscrappers, but after the Chicago fire. While you'll there explore the Newberry Library and City Gallery in Gold Coast which are always free.

Underground Tunnels

The Pedway tour is a mile-long walk that covers a network of underground tunnels and above-ground treasures. The tour is offered on Fridays and Saturdays at 2 p.m. You will have an experienced guide who shares their personal stories about the city. There are also many historical buildings on the Pedway. You will also see a church that was built in the 1920s. This tour also includes a short stop at the De-Paul University campus.

Visit Riverwalk and Lower Wacker Drive

While not entirely underground, the Riverwalk and Lower Wacker Drive provide unique views of the city's infrastructure and the hidden underbelly of downtown Chicago. You can walk along the Riverwalk and explore the area beneath Upper Wacker Drive for free.

The Art Institute of Chicago

The Art Institute of Chicago is one of the city's most renowned cultural institutions, housing an extensive collection of art spanning various periods and styles. Here's a guide to visiting the Art Institute of Chicago, including admission prices:

- **Location:** 111 S Michigan Ave, Chicago, IL 60603
General Admission Prices (As of my last update in January 2022):
  - **Adults (ages 18-64):** $25-30 (prices vary depending on the time of year and ticket type)
  - Seniors (ages 65+): $19-24 (prices vary)
  - Students (with a valid ID): $19-24 (prices vary)
  - Children (ages 14-17): $19-24 (prices vary)
  - Children under 14: Free
  - **Chicago Residents (with proof of residency):** Free on specific days and evenings. Check the museum's website for details.
  - Members: Free

Tips for Visiting the Art Institute of Chicago:
- **Free Days:** The Art Institute offers free admission to Illinois residents on certain days and evenings throughout the year. Check the museum's website for the latest schedule.
- **CityPASS:** Consider purchasing a Chicago CityPASS, which includes admission to the Art Institute of Chicago along with other top attractions in the city. CityPASS can save you money if you plan to visit multiple attractions.
Website: Chicago CityPASS

- **Audio Guides:** The museum offers audio guides that provide additional insights into the artworks and exhibitions. Consider renting one to enhance your visit.
- **Bank of America Museums on Us:** If you have a Bank of America or Merrill Lynch credit or debit card, you can enjoy free admission to several Chicago museums during the first full weekend of each month as part of the Museums on Us program.

Best Free Museums

Chicago offers several free museums and cultural institutions that allow visitors to explore art, history, and more without any admission fees. Here are some of the best free museums in Chicago:

- **National Museum of Mexican Art:** This museum in the Pilsen neighborhood showcases Mexican art and culture. It features a diverse collection of folk art, paintings, sculptures, and rotating exhibitions.
  Website: National Museum of Mexican Art
- **Smart Museum of Art:** Located on the University of Chicago campus, the Smart Museum houses a collection of over 15,000 objects, including European, Asian, and contemporary art. Admission is always free.
  Website: Smart Museum of Art
- **Museum of Contemporary Photography:** Part of Columbia College Chicago, this museum is dedicated to contemporary photography. It offers rotating exhibitions featuring works by emerging and established artists.
  Website: Museum of Contemporary Photography
- **National Hellenic Museum:** Explore the rich history and culture of Greece and Greek Americans at this museum in Chicago's Greektown neighborhood. Free admission days are available.
  Website: National Hellenic Museum
- **International Museum of Surgical Science:** Discover the history of surgery and medical instruments in a historic mansion overlooking Lake Michigan. The museum offers free admission on Tuesdays.
  Website: International Museum of Surgical Science

- **DuSable Museum of African American History:** While the DuSable Museum typically charges admission, Illinois residents can enjoy free admission on certain days. The museum focuses on African American history and culture.
Website: DuSable Museum
- **The Oriental Institute Museum:** Located on the University of Chicago campus, this museum explores the art, archaeology, and history of the ancient Near East. Admission is free, but donations are appreciated.
Website: Oriental Institute
- **Clarke House Museum:** As Chicago's oldest house, the Clarke House Museum offers a glimpse into the city's history. Guided tours are free, but reservations are recommended.
Website: Clarke House Museum
- **Chinese-American Museum of Chicago:** Discover the contributions of Chinese Americans to Chicago's history and culture. The museum offers free admission on Tuesdays.
Website: Chinese-American Museum
- **Smith Museum of Stained Glass Windows:** Located in Chicago's Navy Pier, this museum features a stunning collection of stained glass windows from various periods. Admission is free.
Website: Smith Museum of Stained Glass Windows

Do a self-guided Gangster tour of Chicago

A gangster tour will set you back $30 to $70 in Chicago. Here's a DIY and totally free self-guided gangster tour:

- **Lincoln Park:** Visit the Lincoln Park neighborhood, where the infamous St. Valentine's Day Massacre occurred in 1929. Although the building where the massacre took place no longer exists, you can visit the site, which is located at 2122 N. Clark Street, and see the historical marker.
- **Biograph Theater:** Head to the Biograph Theater at 2433 N. Lincoln Avenue, where John Dillinger was shot and killed by FBI agents in 1934. The theater still stands, and you can take a photo of the historic building.
- **The Green Mill Cocktail Lounge:** This historic jazz club, located at 4802 N. Broadway, was a favorite hangout of Al Capone. While there may be a cover charge for live music, you can still visit during the day to see the club's vintage interior.
- **Cicero:** Take a drive or public transit to the nearby suburb of Cicero, which was a hotbed of gangster activity during the Prohibition era. While there, you can see historic locations associated with Al Capone and other gangsters.
- **Union Station:** Chicago Union Station, located at 225 S. Canal Street, was used by gangsters as a major transportation hub. It's an iconic train station and a piece of Chicago's gangster history.

- **Chicago Riverwalk:** Stroll along the Chicago Riverwalk, which offers beautiful views of the city's architecture. This area was once frequented by gangsters, and you can learn about the city's history as you walk.
- **Public Library:** Visit the Harold Washington Library Center at 400 S. State Street. While there, you can explore the library's extensive collection of books and resources related to Chicago's organized crime.

Gangster History Timeline

1. Prohibition Era:
   - The 1920s and early 1930s marked the Prohibition era when the production and sale of alcoholic beverages were illegal in the United States.
   - Chicago became a hotspot for bootlegging, with various crime syndicates, including the Chicago Outfit led by Al Capone, controlling the illicit alcohol trade.
   - The St. Valentine's Day Massacre in 1929, where seven members of the rival North Side Gang were brutally murdered, is one of the most infamous events of this era.
2. Al Capone:
   - Al Capone, also known as "Scarface," is one of the most notorious gangsters in Chicago's history. He rose to power during Prohibition, controlling illegal alcohol, speakeasies, and various criminal enterprises.
   - Capone's empire made him a wealthy and influential figure in Chicago, but he was eventually convicted of tax evasion in 1931 and sent to prison.
3. Chicago Outfit:
   - The Chicago Outfit is the name commonly used to refer to the Italian-American organized crime syndicate that operated in Chicago.

- Led by figures like Al Capone, Tony Accardo, and Sam Giancana, the Outfit had a significant influence on the city's criminal activities for decades.

4. Corruption and Politics:
  - Chicago had a history of political corruption, with some city officials and law enforcement officers allegedly working in cahoots with gangsters.
  - The "City That Works" reputation often had darker connotations, as it was seen as a place where organized crime could operate relatively openly.

5. Decline of the Outfit:
  - Over time, the Chicago Outfit's power waned due to law enforcement efforts, rivalries, and internal strife.
  - Key members were imprisoned or killed, leading to a decline in the organization's influence.

Visit Garfield Park Conservatory

Located on the west side of Chicago, the Garfield Park Conservatory is an amazing botanical garden. Located just outside of downtown, this free space is perfect for families and couples looking for a fun and relaxing day.

With over two acres of greenhouse space and an outdoor section spanning over 12 acres, the Garfield Park Conservatory is one of the largest in the country. There are nine different rooms and two acres of indoor space, allowing for plenty of exploration. The conservatory features a wide array of plants that are different from those found in the wild. The conservatory also offers educational programs that are open to adults and children. These programs include family programs, school field trips, fundraisers and special events. The conservatory also offers a number of themed rooms and gardens. The Fern Room is home to lush ferns and rock outcrops, while the Palm House shelters graceful palms.

The conservatory is also a great place to visit in the winter. There is a large pond with koi fish and Chihuly glass art pieces. It also offers a looped path with streams and stepping stones.

The conservatory is open 365 days a year. However, it is recommended that visitors arrive at least five minutes before their reservation.

Visit a Sky Chapel

400 feet above street level on the Loop is an the impressive space is the First United Methodist Church surrounded by colorful stained-glass windows and intricate carvings. They offer Free guided tours are available Tuesday through Saturday at 2pm, as well as Sundays at 9:45am and 12:15pm.

'Visit' Wrigley Field for free

Wrigley Field is a 100-year-old baseball park. Get a beer and a hotdog and head to 'knothole gate' a garage-door-sized opening on to the pitch on Sheffield Ave to watch for free.

Discover Truly hidden gems in Chicago

Chicago is a city filled with hidden gems that may not be as widely known but offer unique and authentic experiences. Here are some truly hidden gems in Chicago:

- Alfred Caldwell Lily Pool:
    - Tucked away in Lincoln Park, this serene and secluded garden designed by landscape architect Alfred Caldwell is a peaceful oasis in the heart of the city.

- The Charnley-Persky House:
    - Designed by architects Louis Sullivan and Frank Lloyd Wright, this architectural gem is often overlooked. It offers guided tours showcasing its innovative design.

- Graceland Cemetery:
    - This cemetery is not just a final resting place but also an outdoor sculpture garden with beautiful monuments, statues, and historical significance.

- Oriental Institute Museum:
    - Part of the University of Chicago, this museum houses a remarkable collection of artifacts from ancient civilizations, including Egypt, Mesopotamia, and Persia.
    -
- The International Houses of Chicago:
    - These unique residences offer cultural and intellectual exchanges, hosting events, lec-

tures, and gatherings where you can meet people from around the world.

- Frank Lloyd Wright's Robie House:
  - While some of Wright's designs are well-known, the Robie House in Hyde Park is a masterpiece of Prairie School architecture and offers insightful guided tours.

  -

- Garfield Park Conservatory's Fern Room:
  - While the entire conservatory is beautiful, the Fern Room is particularly enchanting, resembling a prehistoric paradise with lush greenery.

- Chicago French Market:
  - An indoor market featuring a variety of vendors offering international foods, pastries, and unique products, it's a culinary delight off the beaten path.

Relax in Chicago's Parks

Millennium Park:

Park Highlights: Millennium Park is famous for the iconic "Cloud Gate" sculpture (The Bean), Jay Pritzker Pavilion, and beautiful gardens.

Cheap Eats Nearby: Check out food trucks along Michigan Avenue or visit the Park Grill for affordable options. Nearby, you'll also find fast-food chains and casual dining spots.

Grant Park:
> **Park Highlights:** Grant Park is home to Buckingham Fountain, beautiful gardens, and the Museum Campus with attractions like the Field Museum and Shedd Aquarium.

Cheap Eats Nearby: Head to the nearby South Loop neighborhood for affordable options. Giordano's and Lou Malnati's are famous for Chicago-style pizza and often have budget-friendly lunch specials.

Lincoln Park:
Park Highlights: Lincoln Park features a zoo, gardens, and the North Avenue Beach with fantastic views of the city skyline.
Cheap Eats Nearby: The nearby Lincoln Park neighborhood offers numerous dining options. Visit Clark Street for affordable restaurants and cafes. Also, try the Original Rainbow Cone for a classic treat.

Humboldt Park:
Park Highlights: Humboldt Park is known for its large lagoon, gardens, and the historic Humboldt Park Stables.
Cheap Eats Nearby: Head to the nearby neighborhoods of Humboldt Park and Logan Square for a variety of affordable dining options. You'll find taquerias, casual diners, and ethnic restaurants.

Washington Square Park:
Park Highlights: This small park in the Gold Coast neighborhood is a pleasant place to relax.
Cheap Eats Nearby: Explore the nearby Gold Coast area for budget-friendly dining options. You can find affordable delis, pizza places, and cafes.

Wicker Park:
Park Highlights: Wicker Park has a beautiful garden and is surrounded by the trendy Wicker Park and Bucktown neighborhoods.
Cheap Eats Nearby: Explore Division Street and Milwaukee Avenue for a wide range of budget-friendly dining options, including taco joints, dive bars, and quick-service restaurants.

Garfield Park:
   Park Highlights: Garfield Park features lush gardens, a conservatory, and cultural events.
   Cheap Eats Nearby: Head to the nearby West Side neighborhoods for affordable dining. Try soul food restaurants, BBQ joints, and local diners.

Maggie Daley Park:
   Park Highlights: Maggie Daley Park offers a unique playground, mini-golf, and ice skating in the winter.
   Cheap Eats Nearby: Visit the nearby Millennium Park area for affordable food options, including food trucks and casual eateries.

Bike the Lakefront Trail

I did this with a bicycle I rented at Millennium Park for $3. With Lake Michigan in front of you and the Chicago skyline behind, it's a wonderful way to spend an afternoon. There are restrooms and water fountains at various parks and facilities along the trail.

Have a Beach Day

Oak Street Beach is located on North Lake Shore Drive on the shore of Lake Michigan. You can walk there in under 15 minutes from the Magnificent Mile.

There are a few affordable indoor public pools in Chicago, along with their general admission prices:

Humboldt Park Pool:
- Adults (18-64): $5
- Youth (6-17): $2
- Seniors (65+): $2
- Children (under 5): Free
- Holstein Park Pool:
  - Adults (18-64): $5
  - Youth (6-17): $2
  - Seniors (65+): $2
  - Children (under 5): Free
- Morgan Park Sports Center:
  - Adults (18-64): $7

- Youth (6-17): $5
- Seniors (65+): $5
- Children (under 5): Free
- Norwood Park Pool:
  - Adults (18-64): $5
  - Youth (6-17): $2
  - Seniors (65+): $2
  - Children (under 5): Free
- Pulaski Park Pool:
  - Adults (18-64): $5
  - Youth (6-17): $2
  - Seniors (65+): $2
  - Children (under 5): Free

Additionally, the Chicago Park District often offers seasonal pool passes or discounts for frequent visitors, so if you plan to visit the pools regularly during the summer, you may want to inquire about these options for potential cost savings.

Explore the Markets

Maxwell Street Market:
- Located in the University Village neighborhood, famous for affordable street food, clothing, electronics, and more.
- Open every Sunday, offering bargains on a wide range of items, including international foods and vintage goods.

61st Street Farmers Market:
- Located in the Woodlawn neighborhood, offering fresh produce, artisanal products, and prepared foods.
- Focuses on providing affordable, locally sourced, and organic options.

Division Street Farmers Market:
- Located in the Gold Coast neighborhood, operates on Saturdays during the summer.
- Offers reasonably priced fruits, vegetables, baked goods, and other local products.

South Loop Farmers Market:
- Situated in the South Loop neighborhood, features vendors selling fresh produce, artisan foods, and handmade products.
- Operates on select Thursdays during the summer months.

Harrison Street Market:
- Located in the Oak Park Arts District, just outside of Chicago.
- Offers affordable vintage items, handmade crafts, and antiques, making it a great place to find unique, budget-friendly treasures.

Discount Stores:
- Look for discount stores like Aldi, Dollar General, and Family Dollar.
- Known for offering lower prices on groceries and household essentials.

Ethnic Neighborhood Markets:
- Explore the diverse neighborhoods of Chicago, such as Chinatown, Little Italy, or Mexican neighborhoods like Pilsen and Little Village.

Workout for Free

Get a workout in for free in Chicago. LA Fitness offers a Free 3day guest pass including pool and sauna/ steam rooms. I wouldn't mention anything about travelling through. They are offering you the pass for free to convert you into a paying member. Don't feel bad, think of all the money you've paid gyms and never used their services. You can also leave them a review online if you feel bad for using their facilities for free.

Here are more free workout options:

1.   **Chicago Park District:** The Chicago Park District offers a variety of free fitness classes and wellness pro-grams at parks throughout the city. These classes may include yoga, Zumba, Pilates, and more. Check the Chicago Park District's website or visit your local park for schedules and locations.
2.   **Millennium Park:** Millennium Park frequently hosts free fitness events and classes during the summer months. These classes may include yoga, Tai Chi, and Pilates. Check the Millennium Park website or event list-ings for details.
3.   **Chicago Riverwalk:** The Chicago Riverwalk often hosts free fitness classes, such as yoga and cardio workouts, during the summer. Keep an eye on their event schedule for updates.
4.   **Lululemon:** Some Lululemon stores in Chicago offer free weekly yoga or fitness classes. Check with your local Lululemon store for their class schedule.
5.   **Athleta:** Athleta stores occasionally offer free fitness classes and events, including yoga and workout classes. Check the Athleta website or contact the store near you for details.

Free Live Music

Chicago is home to some of the best free live music you will ever hear. Here are the greats.

Green Mill Cocktail Lounge: Located in the Uptown neighborhood, the Green Mill is an iconic jazz club that has been a Chicago institution for decades. They often host free early evening jazz performances and have a cozy atmosphere.

Andy's Jazz Club: Andy's Jazz Club, located in the River North area, is known for its live jazz performances. They offer free admission for certain sets, usually earlier in the evening.

Kingston Mines: Kingston Mines is a legendary Chicago blues club in the Lincoln Park neighborhood. They frequently have free early evening shows in one of their two stages. It's a great place to experience authentic Chicago blues.

The California Clipper: This Humboldt Park bar features live music several nights a week, including jazz, soul, and rockabilly. Some shows are free, but there may be a small cover charge for certain performances.

The Hideout: The Hideout, located in the Bucktown neighborhood, is known for its eclectic live music lineup, featuring indie rock, folk, and experimental acts. While some shows have a cover charge, they often host free performances as well.

The Old Town School of Folk Music: While primarily a music school, the Old Town School of Folk Music also hosts free concerts and events, showcasing a variety of folk and world music genres. Check their calendar for free shows.

Reggie's Music Joint: Reggie's, in the South Loop, offers a mix of live music genres, including rock, punk, and metal. They have free and low-cost shows, especially earlier in the evening.

The Gallery Cabaret: This Bucktown bar features live music, open mic nights, and other performances. Many of their events are free, and it's a great place to discover local talent.

Uncommon Ground: With two locations in Chicago, Uncommon Ground often hosts free live music performances, including singer-songwriters and indie bands. They're known for their commitment to sustainability and locally sourced food.

The Red Line Tap: Located in the Rogers Park neighborhood, the Red Line Tap hosts live music events, including rock, blues, and indie acts. Some shows are free, while others may have a small cover charge.

Explore Street Art

Chicago has a huge array of colorful murals and graffiti art displayed throughout the city. Murals sometimes cover up entire buildings and symbolize recent and historical events and topics. The best places to explore are:

- **Pilsen:** Pilsen is arguably Chicago's street art mecca. The neighborhood is known for its vibrant murals, colorful graffiti, and artistic culture. Walk along 18th Street, especially near the Pilsen Mural Wall at 16th and Blue Island, to see some of the most striking street art in the city.
- **Wicker Park and Bucktown:** These neighboring neighborhoods are filled with artistic energy. Stroll along Damen Avenue, Milwaukee Avenue, and North Avenue to discover a wide range of street art, from large murals to smaller pieces on storefronts and utility boxes.
- **Logan Square:** Logan Square is another hotspot for street art. Explore the areas around Milwaukee Avenue and Logan Boulevard to find impressive murals and cre-

ative installations that reflect the neighborhood's artistic spirit.

- **South Loop:** The South Loop neighborhood has been transforming with the addition of street art, thanks to events like the Wabash Arts Corridor. Walk around the Roosevelt Collection Shops and Printer's Row to see captivating street art.
- **Hyde Park:** Hyde Park on the South Side has its share of street art, often reflecting the area's cultural diversity. You can find murals and artwork along 53rd Street and throughout the neighborhood.
- **Wabash Arts Corridor:** This is a concentrated area in the South Loop filled with street art and murals. It's a designated arts district with large-scale murals that are constantly evolving.
- **The 606/Bloomingdale Trail:** This elevated trail on Chicago's Northwest Side features public art installations and murals along its path. It offers a unique way to explore street art while enjoying a scenic walk or bike ride.
- **West Town:** The West Town neighborhood, which includes Ukrainian Village and East Village, has a growing street art scene. Wander through its residential streets to discover various murals and graffiti art.
- **Edgewater:** Located on the North Side, Edgewater has its own share of street art. Explore the area around Granville Avenue and Broadway Street to find colorful murals and art installations.
- **Street Festivals:** Keep an eye out for street festivals and events like the Wicker Park Fest, Logan Square Arts Festival, and others. These events often feature live mural painting and street art exhibitions.
- **Chicago Riverwalk:** The Chicago Riverwalk has seen an increase in street art and public art installations in recent years. Explore this scenic area along the Chicago River to discover unique outdoor art pieces.

Go Thrift Shopping

Chicago offers a variety of thrift stores where you can find insanely cheap clothing, furniture, and more. The prices may vary depending on the store and the items, but here are some thrift stores in Chicago known for their super cheap prices:

- **Village Discount Outlet:** With multiple locations in Chicago, Village Discount Outlet is known for its low prices on clothing, shoes, and household items. They frequently have sales and discount days.
- **Goodwill:** Goodwill has several locations throughout Chicago, offering a wide range of thrifted goods at budget-friendly prices. They often have special discount days.
- **Salvation Army Family Store:** The Salvation Army thrift stores in Chicago offer clothing, furniture, and household items at affordable prices. Look out for their weekly sales.
- **Unique Thrift Store:** Unique Thrift Store has several locations in Chicago and is known for its vast selection of clothing, accessories, and home goods at reasonable prices.
- **Brown Elephant Resale Shops:** Operated by Howard Brown Health, these thrift shops offer clothing, furniture, and unique finds. The prices are generally affordable, and your purchases support a good cause.
- **Ragstock:** Ragstock in Wicker Park offers a mix of vintage and thrifted clothing, including unique and trendy items at budget-friendly prices.
- **Crossroads Trading Co.:** While not a traditional thrift store, Crossroads Trading Co. in Wicker Park offers secondhand clothing and accessories at lower prices than many retail stores.

- **The Ark Thrift Shop:** Located in Lincoln Park, The Ark Thrift Shop offers gently used clothing, furniture, and housewares at competitive prices.
- **Eco Thrift:** Eco Thrift in Edgewater specializes in eco-friendly and sustainable clothing and home goods, often at affordable prices.
- **Savers:** Located in the nearby suburb of Niles, Savers is a thrift superstore with a wide selection of secondhand items at competitive prices.

Free Things to Do at Night in Chicago

Chicago offers a variety of free nighttime activities and events for those looking to enjoy the city after the sun goes down. Here are some options:

- Millennium Park:
    - Visit Millennium Park at night to see iconic landmarks like the Cloud Gate sculpture (a.k.a. "The Bean") illuminated. It's a beautiful and free experience.
- Navy Pier Fireworks:
    - During the summer months, Navy Pier often hosts free fireworks displays on Wednesday and Saturday evenings. Check the schedule for dates and times.
- Chicago Cultural Center:
    - Attend free concerts, film screenings, lectures, and art exhibitions at the Chicago Cultural

Center, which frequently hosts evening events.

- Stroll Along the Lakefront:
    - Take a leisurely walk or bike ride along Chicago's Lakefront Trail. The skyline views are especially stunning at night.
- Chicago Riverwalk:
    - Explore the Chicago Riverwalk, which remains open in the evening. It's a scenic spot for a nighttime stroll.
- Free Music Events:
    - Keep an eye out for free live music events and outdoor concerts in parks and public spaces, especially during the summer months.
- Parks and Beaches:
    - Many of Chicago's parks and beaches remain open at night. Bring a blanket and enjoy stargazing, a picnic, or a late-night swim in designated areas.
- Chicago Public Library Events:
    - Some Chicago Public Library branches host evening events, including book readings, author talks, and discussions.
- Art Galleries and Openings:
    - Attend art gallery openings and exhibitions, often featuring free wine and snacks, in neighborhoods like Pilsen and Wicker Park.
- Neighborhood Festivals:
    - Some neighborhoods host free evening festivals, showcasing local culture, food, and music. Check local event listings for details.
- Free Comedy Shows:
    - Several comedy clubs in Chicago offer free or low-cost open mic nights. Enjoy a night of laughter without breaking the bank.
- Chicago's Neighborhoods:

- Explore neighborhoods like Wicker Park, Logan Square, and Lakeview, which have vibrant nightlife scenes and free events.
- Cityscape Views:
  - Visit rooftop bars or elevated public spaces like the 360 Chicago Observation Deck or The Signature Lounge for cityscape views. While drinks may be pricey, the views are free.
- Beach Bonfires:
  - Some Chicago beaches permit bonfires during certain hours. Check the regulations and enjoy a beach bonfire with friends.
- Walking Tours:
  - Take a self-guided walking tour through neighborhoods like the Historic Pullman District or explore Chicago's street art scene in Pilsen.

Watch Free comedy

There's an abundance of free stand-up comedy in Chicago.

1.   **The Playground Theater:** The Playground Theater in the Lakeview neighborhood hosts free improv shows, sketch comedy, and open mic nights.
2.   **ComedySportz Chicago:** ComedySportz offers family-friendly improv comedy shows with two teams competing in various comedic games. While there's usually an admission fee, they occasionally offer free shows or discounted tickets on specific nights.
3.   **Cole's Bar:** Cole's Bar in the Logan Square neighborhood hosts the "Comedians You Should Know" showcase, which features local and nationally recognized comedians. The show typically has no cover charge.
4.   **Gman Tavern:** Located in Wrigleyville, Gman Tavern hosts free comedy shows, including the "Parlour Car Comedy" showcase, which features a mix of local and touring comedians.

5.   **Comedy Open Mic Nights:** Many comedy clubs and bars in Chicago host open mic nights, where aspiring comedians try out new material. While the quality can vary, these events are often free to attend. Some popular open mic nights include the Laugh Factory's "Chicago's Best Stand-Up" and "Shithole."

6.   **Zanies Comedy Clubs:** While Zanies is a well-known comedy club chain with paid shows, they occasionally offer free preview shows featuring up-and-coming comedians. Check their schedule for any free or low-cost events.

7.   **Second City Training Center:** The Second City Training Center often hosts free student showcases and improv jams, allowing you to see emerging comedic talent.

8.   **The Hideout:** The Hideout in the Bucktown neighborhood occasionally hosts free comedy shows, including the "Shame That Tune" comedy game show.

Escape the Crowds

2.7M residents call 234 square miles of land home. When it all gets too much here are 20 such places in Chicago:

- **North Park Village Nature Center:** This nature preserve on the city's Northwest Side offers hiking trails, wetlands, and birdwatching opportunities in a tranquil setting.
- **Jackson Park's Japanese Garden:** Find tranquility in this beautifully landscaped Japanese garden, complete with a serene pond and colorful foliage.
- **Promontory Point:** This lakefront park in Hyde Park offers stunning views of Lake Michigan and a peaceful atmosphere away from the city's hustle and bustle.
- **Montrose Point Bird Sanctuary:** Located on the North Side, this sanctuary is a haven for birdwatchers with its diverse bird population and scenic views.
- **Glessner House Museum Gardens:** Explore the historic home's peaceful garden in the Prairie Avenue Historic District for a glimpse into Chicago's architectural history.
- **Northerly Island:** Escape to this man-made peninsula in the heart of the city for hiking, birdwatching, and beautiful views of the Chicago skyline.
- **Northwestern University's Evanston Campus:** Just north of Chicago, the Evanston campus offers a quieter atmosphere with lovely architecture and lakefront access.
- **Chicago Botanic Garden:** While slightly outside the city, this garden in Glencoe is a tranquil escape with beautiful landscapes, gardens, and walking paths.

- **The 606/Bloomingdale Trail:** Enjoy a leisurely walk or bike ride along this elevated trail on the city's Northwest Side, away from busy streets.
- **Loyola University's Lakeshore Campus:** Visit the serene campus in the Rogers Park neighborhood, with lakefront access and peaceful spots to relax.
- **Garfield Park Conservatory:** This urban oasis on the West Side offers free admission and a lush, tropical environment to explore at your own pace.
- **North Pond Nature Sanctuary:** Discover a quiet natural area within Lincoln Park, featuring a pond, boardwalks, and a variety of birdlife.
- **Humboldt Park's Lagoon:** Humboldt Park offers a peaceful lagoon surrounded by gardens, perfect for a relaxing stroll or a picnic.
- **The Money Museum at the Federal Reserve Bank:** Explore the history of currency in a quieter setting, and learn about the economy in a unique way.
- **International Museum of Surgical Science:** This museum in a historic mansion in Lincoln Park provides a unique and serene atmosphere for those interested in medical history.
- **Nature Boardwalk at Lincoln Park Zoo:** While the zoo itself can be crowded, the adjacent nature boardwalk offers a quieter space for contemplation.
- **Roger Williams Park:** Located in the Rogers Park neighborhood, this park offers a peaceful retreat with gardens, trails, and a lagoon.
- **Ping Tom Memorial Park:** Located in Chinatown, this park along the Chicago River features walking paths, green spaces, and a peaceful ambiance.

- **Edgewater Beach:** The northernmost beach in Chicago, Edgewater Beach offers a quieter alternative to the more popular lakefront beaches.

Not Super Cheap but Loved

Skydeck Chicago - Willis Tower:
General Admission: Adults (ages 12-64) - $30.50, Youth (ages 3-11) - $22.00, Children under 3 - Free
The Tilt Experience (optional): $15.00 in addition to general admission

Museum of Science and Industry:
General Admission: Adults - $21.95, Children (ages 3-11) - $12.95, Children under 3 - Free
Special exhibitions and experiences may have additional fees.

Shedd Aquarium:
General Admission (Shedd Pass): Adults - $39.95, Children (ages 3-11) - $29.95, Children under 3 - Free
Special passes and experiences may have additional fees.

Adler Planetarium:
General Admission (Anytime Pass): Adults - $40.00, Children (ages 3-11) - $35.00, Children under 3 - Free
Special exhibitions and sky shows may have additional fees.

360 CHICAGO - John Hancock Observatory:
General Admission: Adults - $28.00, Youth (ages 3-11) - $22.00, Children under 3 - Free
The Tilt Experience (optional): $7.00 in addition to general admission

Food and drink Hacks

The tastiest food in Chicago

Cinnamon rolls from Anne Sathers, Donuts from Do-Rite and Stan's, Cheese fries and Italian beef from Portillos, Acai bowls from Hi-Vibe, Bubble tea from Te Amo and affordable sushi from Ryo, brunch at the bongo room.

Try Chicken Vesuvio

This dish is a traditional Italian recipe that is usually served at almost every Italian restaurant in the Windy City. Chicken Vesuvio is served with white wine sauce and peas. Those who prefer a traditional Italian beef sandwich should try the Italian beef Chicago sandwich, which features a crusty Italian roll piled high with thinly sliced roast beef. It also comes with an au jus sauce and choice of peppers.

Garrett's popcorn

Another Chicago food that's hard to miss is Garrett's popcorn. This Chicago favorite has been serving up signature blue-striped tins for nearly 60 years. The popcorn is so good, in fact, that it's considered one of the best snacks in the city.

Parachute Cheeseburger

Another popular Chicago food is the Parachute Cheeseburger. This dish is made with bacon, cheese, and scallions. It's the most popular item on the menu at Au Cheval, a popular restaurant in Wicker Park. It's also served at Navy Pier.

Try Old Fashioned Donuts

Located in Roseland, Old Fashioned Donuts has served the community for over forty years. Open daily for breakfast and lunch, the shop has been featured in many food magazines. Their doughnuts are made from scratch, and they also offer takeout. Founded by Buritt Bulloch and his wife Mamie, the shop opened in 1972. Today, Old Fashioned Donuts offers a variety of flavors, including apple fritters. Old Fashioned Donuts offers over forty flavors. In addition to classic favorites, like chocolate cake donuts and chocolate glaze doughnuts, they also offer apple fritters, gluten free varieties, and Texas doughnuts, which are big enough to fit your arm.
The owner, Burritt Bulloch, has never missed a day of work. He starts his day at five a.m., and he usually makes his first batch of doughnuts in the shop window.

Free coffee refills

Need a coffee after learning all that Chicago history? Head to Intelligentsia Coffee or Two Hearted also offer unlimited refills, great if you need a laptop day.

BYOBs.

Bring your own liquor 2 dinner and save money. Heres a few BYOB restaurnts: Tango Sur. Diva sushi which always has deals on Groupon. Seadog and Cozy Noodle.

Use Opentable

OpenTable.com helps guide you through choosing the type of food you want, the specific restaurant and then lets you book a table according to date and time based on availability and with discounts.

Cheap Speakeasies

Speakeasies in Chicago can offer a unique and often retro experience, but they are not always known for being the cheapest places to enjoy a drink. However, here are a few speakeasy-style bars in Chicago that are known for their relatively affordable prices:

- **The Library at Gilt Bar:** Located in the River North neighborhood, this speakeasy-style bar is hidden behind a bookcase inside Gilt Bar. While it's not the cheapest option, it offers reasonably priced cocktails in an elegant atmosphere.
- **The Violet Hour:** Known for its craft cocktails, The Violet Hour in Wicker Park offers a happy hour menu with discounted drinks, making it a bit more budget-friendly during those hours.
- **The Drifter:** This intimate, underground speakeasy beneath the Green Door Tavern in River North often features live jazz music and a rotating menu of reasonably priced cocktails.
- **Three Dots and a Dash:** While it's more of a tiki bar than a traditional speakeasy, Three Dots and a Dash in River North offers some affordable drink options during happy hour and special events.
- **Untitled Supper Club:** This upscale establishment in River North has a hidden, vintage-inspired speakeasy on its lower level. While not the cheapest option, it occasionally offers special promotions and discounts on drinks.

Best All You Can Eat Restaurants in Chicago

Chicago has a variety of all-you-can-eat restaurants that cater to different tastes and budgets. Here are some popular all-you-can-eat options with price ranges:

1. Brazilian Steakhouse (Churrascaria):
   * Experience a meat lover's paradise with a continuous flow of grilled meats brought to your table. Prices can vary but typically range from $40 to $60 or more per person for dinner. Some well-known Brazilian steakhouses in Chicago include Fogo de Chão, Texas de Brazil, and Chama Gaúcha.
2. Korean BBQ:
   * Enjoy all-you-can-eat Korean BBQ, which includes a variety of marinated meats, side dishes, and vegetables for grilling. Lunch prices often range from $15 to $30 per person, while dinner prices can range from $25 to $45 or more. Popular spots include San Soo Gab San, Gogi, and Iron Age.
3. Sushi Buffet:
   * Satisfy your sushi cravings with all-you-can-eat sushi, sashimi, and rolls. Prices typically start around $20 for lunch and $30 for dinner per person. Some options include Sushi Para, Sushi Plus, and Sakura Sushi & Grill.

Cheap Eats - Mains under $10

Street food can be a hard thing to find in Chicago, but laws are changing and you can find food trucks around The Loop now. If you want a sit-down meal, fill your stomach without emptying your wallet by trying these local restaurants with mains under $10.

(Download the offline map on google maps, (instructions 1. go to app 2. select offline apps in the left sidebar 3. go to the area you want to download 4. click download). Then simply type the restaurant names in to navigate, star them so you can see where the cheap eats are when you're out and about to avoid wasting your money at hyped tourist joints)

Redhot Ranch
No-frills spot offering hot dogs, burgers and fries in a counter-serve space with outdoor seating.

Pierogi Heaven
Good, no frills, simple and cheap Polish food.

Aloha Eats
Great affordable Hawaiian food.

Sultan's Market
Very affordable, unpretentious, and delicious food. Outdoor seating

Birrieria Zaragoza
Great Mexican with amazing tacos.

Cemitas Puebla
Poblano fare including cemitas (Mexican sandwiches) and chalupas. They have Happy hour drinks · Comfort food and Outdoor seating.

En Hakkore Bibimbap and Taco
Great Korean food that is fresh and relatively cheap.

U.B. Dogs
Classic weekday-only counter for steamed Chicago-style beef hot dogs and housemade burgers.

Nhu Lan Bakery
Shop offering Vietnamese fare and smoothies, including banh mi and pho, with vegetarian options.

Del Seoul
Great quality Korean for a very a low price.

bopNgrillorean
Counter-serve joint for creative burgers with Korean and other global ingredients and Asian rice plates.

Chiu Quon Bakery & Dim Sum Bakery
Amazing egg custard and sweet top buns for low prices. One of the best bakeries in Chicago.

Fatso's Last Stand
Hamburger · 2258 W Chicago Ave
Hot dog stand with late hours weekendsIf you are planning on a low cost high quality meal EAT HERE

Sultan's Market
Middle Eastern · 2057 W North Ave

Quick-serve Middle Eastern fare. Cash only, cheap eats spot.

Seoul Taco
Restaurant · 738 N Clark St
Korean-Mexican street food cafe. On the cheaper side, and the food is great

Chicago Lunchbox
Asian Fusion · 400 S Financial Pl
Unfussy pick for Asian fusion fare

Carnitas Uruapan Restaurant
Mexican · 1725 W 18th St
Mainstay for Mexican street food. The best place to eat carnitas and cheap

Nhu Lan Bakery
Bakery · 2612 W Lawrence Ave
Quick stop for Vietnamese fare & drinks

Cafecito
Cuban · 7 N Wells St
Cuban coffee shop for pressed sandwiches
Good sandwiches at cheap prices

BienMeSabe Venezuelan Arepa Bar
Venezuelan · 29 E Adams St
Modern stop for simple and cheap Venezuelan fare.

Margie's Candies
Address: 1960 N Western Ave
Old-fashioned ice cream parlor serving the best scoops in Chicago.

Day Trips

Chicago offers a variety of exciting day trip options to explore the surrounding areas and experience diverse attractions. Here are some of the best day trips from Chicago, along with estimated prices:

- Milwaukee, Wisconsin:
  - Distance from Chicago: Approximately 90 miles (144 kilometers).
  - Highlights: Milwaukee Art Museum, Harley-Davidson Museum, Lakefront Brewery.
  - Estimated Costs: Gasoline costs may vary, and admission fees to attractions vary.
- Starved Rock State Park, Illinois:
  - Distance from Chicago: Approximately 100 miles (161 kilometers).
  - Highlights: Hiking, waterfalls, scenic canyons.
  - Estimated Costs: State park entrance fee (around $10 per vehicle) and optional guided activities.
- Galena, Illinois:
  - Distance from Chicago: Approximately 165 miles (266 kilometers).
  - Highlights: Historic town, shopping, Galena Cellars Vineyard & Winery.
  - Estimated Costs: Gasoline costs, dining, shopping expenses, and winery tours.
- Indiana Dunes National Park, Indiana:
  - Distance from Chicago: Approximately 50 miles (80 kilometers).
  - Highlights: Sandy beaches, dune hiking, bird watching.
  - Estimated Costs: State park entrance fee (around $6 per vehicle) and dining expenses.
- Frank Lloyd Wright Tour, Oak Park, Illinois:

- Distance from Chicago: Located within Chicago's western suburbs.
- Highlights: Touring Frank Lloyd Wright's architectural masterpieces.
- Estimated Costs: Guided tour fees (vary depending on the specific tour).
- Lake Geneva, Wisconsin:
  - Distance from Chicago: Approximately 80 miles (129 kilometers).
  - Highlights: Lake Geneva Cruise Line, scenic boat tours, lakeside dining.
  - Estimated Costs: Boat tour fees (starting at around $20) and dining expenses.

Getting Out

Train

Booking ahead can save you up to 60% of the cost of an Amtrak ticket.

Bus

Megabus are the cheapest bus operator from Chicago to Madison, miwaukee, Detroit and a number of other US cities.

BoltBus: BoltBus is a subsidiary of Greyhound and offers competitive fares on popular routes. They often have deals for early bookings.

FlixBus: FlixBus is a European bus company that has expanded to the United States. They offer affordable fares and have routes departing from Chicago to multiple cities.

MegaBusplus: MegaBusplus is a service that combines a Megabus trip with a connecting Amtrak train journey. This option can provide affordable long-distance travel.

Plane

At the time of writing Spirit are offering the cheapest flights onwards.Take advantage of discounts and specials. Sign up for e-newsletters from local carriers including Spirit to learn about special fares. Be careful with cheap airlines, most will allow hand-luggage only, and some charge for anything that is not a backpack. Check their websites before booking if you need to take luggage.

Airport Lounges

You don't need to be flying business or first class to enjoy an airport lounge. Here are three methods you can use to access lounges at Chicago airport:

- Get or use a credit card that gives free lounge access. NerdWallet has a good write-up about cards that offer free lounge access. www.nerdwallet.com/best/credit-cards/airport-lounge-access

- Buy onetime access. They start at $23 and often include free showers and free drinks and food.

- Find free access with the LoungeBuddy app. You pay an annual fee of $25 to use the app. In practice, the free lounges are heavily concentrated in the United States but it's worth checking their website to see if they have a free lounge in Chicago - www.loungebuddy.com/ at the time of writing they do not.

From	To	Depart	Return
Chicago, IL (Any)	Everywhere	Cheapest mo...	(One Way)
Direct flights only			

Estimated lowest prices only. Found in the last 15 days.

United States	from $20
Canada	from $59
Guatemala	from $59
Mexico	from $60
Peru	from $72
Costa Rica	from $75

Here are the cheapest airport lounges in the windy city:

Swissport Lounges (Chicago O'Hare International Airport - Terminal 5):
- Day Pass: Prices for a single visit day pass are usually around $40 to $50 per person.
- Walk-in Access: Some Swissport lounges offer walk-in access without a membership or day pass, with prices around $45 to $55 per person.

United Club (Chicago O'Hare International Airport - Terminal 1 and Terminal 2):
- Day Pass: Prices typically range from $59 to $69 per person.
- Annual Membership: United Club offers annual membership options with access to United Club lounges worldwide. Prices vary based on membership type and eligibility.

American Airlines Admirals Club (Chicago O'Hare International Airport - Terminal 3):
- Day Pass: Prices for a day pass range from $59 to $75 per person.
- Annual Membership: American Airlines offers annual Admirals Club memberships with varying pricing based on elite status and membership type.

Delta Sky Club (Chicago O'Hare International Airport - Terminal 2):
- Access Fee: Prices for a single visit day pass typically range from $59 to $69 per person.

Tourist Scams to avoid

- **The Broken Camera or Phone Scam:** A person may approach you, claiming that they accidentally bumped into you and broke their camera or phone. They will then ask you for money to repair or replace it. Be cautious and do not give money to strangers.

- **The "Free" CD or Art Scam:** You may encounter individuals on the streets offering you a "free" CD, artwork, or other items. Once you accept it, they will aggressively demand payment for it. Politely decline any unsolicited offers.

- **The Fake Charity Scam:** Some individuals may approach you, claiming to represent a charitable organization and asking for donations. Always verify the legitimacy of the charity and donate through official channels.

- **The Overpriced Taxi Scam:** Be cautious when taking a taxi. Some unscrupulous drivers may take longer routes or charge excessive fares to tourists. Use reputable taxi services or ridesharing apps to ensure fair pricing.

- **The "Helpful" Stranger Scam:** Someone may offer to help you with directions, then demand payment for their assistance. Be cautious when accepting help from strangers and politely decline if you feel uncomfortable.

- **The Fake Parking Attendant Scam:** In some areas, individuals may pose as parking attendants and charge you for parking in a public space. Always use official parking facilities and verify the legitimacy of attendants.

- **The Distraction Pickpocket:** Be aware of your surroundings, especially in crowded places. Thieves may work in teams to distract you while one of them tries to steal your belongings. Keep your valuables secure and be mindful of your personal space.
- **The Street Gambling Scam:** Avoid participating in street gambling games or shell games on the streets, as they are often rigged, and you are likely to lose money.
- **Ticket Scams:** Only purchase tickets for events, attractions, or tours from official sources. Be cautious of individuals selling tickets on the street, as they may be counterfeit.

To avoid falling victim to these scams, it's essential to stay vigilant, trust your instincts, and be cautious when dealing with strangers.

Common Complaints

Complaint 1: The Weather
- Complaint: Chicago is known for its unpredictable weather, with cold winters and hot summers.
- Solution: Dress in layers to adapt to changing temperatures. Invest in a good winter coat and waterproof boots for the winter months. Enjoy indoor activities during extreme weather, such as visiting museums or trying the city's diverse cuisine.

Complaint 2: Traffic and Parking
- Complaint: Traffic congestion and limited parking can be frustrating.
- Solution: Use public transportation or ridesharing services when possible to avoid traffic. Consider living in neighborhoods with better parking options, or use parking apps to find available spots.

Complaint 3: Public Transportation Delays
- Complaint: Delays and service interruptions can occur on Chicago's public transportation.
- Solution: Plan your commute with extra time to account for potential delays. Sign up for transit alerts to stay informed about service disruptions.

Complaint 4: Noise and Crowds
- Complaint: Chicago can be noisy and crowded, especially in popular tourist areas.
- Solution: Seek out quieter neighborhoods, parks, or green spaces for relaxation. Consider noise-cancelling headphones or earplugs for busy areas.

Complaint 4: Local Taxes

Historical events that help you make sense of Chicago

Chicago is shaped by a series of key historical events and milestones. Understanding these events can provide valuable insights into the city's development and character. Here are some historical events that help make sense of Chicago:

- Great Chicago Fire (1871):
    - The Great Chicago Fire was a devastating event that destroyed a significant portion of the city in 1871. It led to the rebuilding of Chicago, with an emphasis on modern urban planning and fire-resistant architecture.
- The Chicago World's Fair (1893):
    - The World's Columbian Exposition of 1893 showcased Chicago as a cultural and technological hub. It introduced innovations such as the Ferris Wheel and inspired the City Beautiful movement, influencing urban planning and architecture.
- The Chicago Race Riots (1919):
    - The 1919 race riots highlighted racial tensions and discrimination in Chicago. This event had a lasting impact on the city's African American community and spurred discussions about civil rights.
- Prohibition and Gangster Era (1920s):
    - Prohibition in the 1920s gave rise to organized crime, with figures like Al Capone dominating the city's underworld. This era left

a mark on Chicago's cultural identity and is depicted in movies and literature.

- Labor Movements and the Haymarket Affair (1886):
  - The Haymarket Affair was a labor protest that turned violent in 1886. It played a role in the labor rights movement and the establishment of Labor Day.
- Chicago Blues and Jazz (20th Century):
  - Chicago has a rich musical heritage, particularly in blues and jazz. It played a pivotal role in the development of these genres, with iconic figures like Muddy Waters and Louis Armstrong.
- Civil Rights Movement and Martin Luther King Jr. (1950s-1960s):
  - Chicago was a battleground for the civil rights movement, with Martin Luther King Jr. leading efforts to end segregation and housing discrimination in the city.
- Democratic National Convention (1968):
  - The 1968 Democratic National Convention in Chicago was marked by protests and clashes with law enforcement. It became a symbol of the anti-war movement and political activism of the era.
- Chicago Bulls Dynasty (1990s):
  - The dominance of the Chicago Bulls in the NBA during the 1990s, led by Michael Jordan, brought international fame to the city and contributed to Chicago's sports culture.
- Modern Architecture and Skyscrapers:
  - Chicago is renowned for its modern architecture and skyscrapers. Key architects like Frank Lloyd Wright, Ludwig Mies van der Rohe, and others left a lasting imprint on the city's skyline.
- Cultural Institutions and Museums:

- The establishment of world-class cultural institutions like the Art Institute of Chicago and the Museum of Science and Industry has solidified the city's reputation as a cultural hub.
- Economic Transformation:
  - Chicago's economic transformation from a meatpacking and manufacturing hub to a global financial center has widen the gap between rich and poor.

Attraction Checklist

Here's a checklist of the top 20 things to do in Chicago

- ☑ Visit Millennium Park and see "The Bean" (Cloud Gate).
- ☑ Explore the Art Institute of Chicago.
- ☑ Take an architecture boat tour on the Chicago River.
- ☑ Enjoy a stroll along Navy Pier.
- ☑ Discover the Shedd Aquarium.
- ☑ Marvel at the views from Skydeck Chicago (Willis Tower).
- ☑ Immerse yourself in history at the Field Museum.
- ☑ Explore the Museum of Science and Industry.
- ☑ Take a walk along the Lakefront Trail.
- ☑ Attend a live performance at The Chicago Theatre.
- ☑ Experience a Chicago-style deep-dish pizza.
- ☑ Cheer for the Chicago Cubs at Wrigley Field.
- ☑ Visit the Lincoln Park Zoo (free admission).
- ☑ Explore the 360 Chicago Observation Deck (formerly John Hancock Center).
- ☑ Take a leisurely bike ride along Lake Michigan.
- ☑ Enjoy the vibrant nightlife in neighborhoods like Wicker Park.
- ☑ Discover the beautiful Garfield Park Conservatory.
- ☑ Visit the historic Robie House by Frank Lloyd Wright.
- ☑ Explore the vibrant neighborhoods of Pilsen and Logan Square.
- ☑ Take in the views from Buckingham Fountain in Grant Park.

Personal Cost Breakdown (3 days in Chicago on a shoestring)

	How	Cost normally/ advice	Cost when following suggested
How I got from the airport to the city	The Blue Line 'L' train $5	$25 Taxi	$5
Where I stayed	Chicago Get away Hostel $10	Hotels are upwards of $150 a	$30
Tastiest street foods I ate and cost	Hotdogs. I'm not a fan of the Chicago pizza, which is more like a pie.	You can pick up a decent hotdog for $6	$6
How I got around	Walked and cycled	Visit from May to be able to	$3
What I saw and paid	Architecture, downtown, museums, free tours,	There's so much to see and do for free. The Arts Institute	$40
My on ward flight	Atlanta with Spirit	Book six weeks ahead for the low-	$20
My Total costs	US$130		US$130

Practical things to remember to save money

Transportation:

Use public transportation: Chicago's public transit system, including buses and the "L" train, is an affordable way to get around the city.

Get a Chicago Transit Authority (CTA) Ventra Card for reduced fares on buses and trains.

Consider walking or biking for short distances, as many attractions are within walking or biking distance in downtown Chicago.

Use rideshare apps like Uber or Lyft, but google for free credit before.

Accommodation:

Blindbook and use day passes to luxury hotels.
Consider Airbnb for a wider range of accommodation options, including rooms in local homes.
Book accommodations in advance to take advantage of early booking discounts.

Dining:

Use too good to go

Explore neighborhood eateries: Venture away from touristy areas to find more affordable restaurants with authentic local cuisine.

Look for happy hour specials: Many bars and restaurants offer discounted drinks and appetizers during happy hours.

Sightseeing and Attractions:

Choose a CityPASS or Go Chicago Card: These cards provide discounted access to multiple attractions, saving you 55% on admissions.

Take advantage of free attractions: Explore free attractions like Millennium Park, Lincoln Park Zoo, and the Chicago Cultural Center.

Use free guided tours: Some organizations offer free walking tours of the city, allowing you to learn about its history without spending extra.

Entertainment and Events:

Use discount websites: Check websites like Groupon or Goldstar for discounted tickets to shows, events, and activities.

Miscellaneous:
Carry a reusable water bottle: Save money on bottled water by filling up your reusable bottle at water fountains throughout the city.

Utilize free Wi-Fi: Many cafes, parks, and public spaces offer free Wi-Fi, reducing the need for expensive data plans.

Money Mistakes

Cost	Impact	Solution
Using your home currency	Some credit card rates charge for every transaction in another currency. Check carefully before you use it	Use a prepaid currency card like Wise Multi-Currency Debit Card.
Buying bottled water	At $1 a botle, this is a cost that can mount up quickly	Refill from the tap. Bring an on the go water filter bottle like Water-to-go.
Not eating at food trucks	**Being Unaware of Tipping Culture**: Tipping is customary in the United States. Failing to tip at restaurants, hotels, or for services can lead to uncomfortable situations or negative experiences.	Dine at food trucks to avoid extra tipping expenses.
Eating like a tourist	Eating at tourist traps can triple your bill. Choose wisely	Star cheap eats on google maps so you're never far from one
Renting a car	Renting a car without considering parking fees, traffic, and gas expenses can be costly.	Chicago has an extensive public transportation system, including buses and the "L" train.
Always look for a coupon on everything	Chicago has a high sales tax rate, look for coupons or thrift shop.	super easy to do with a quick google search.

RECAP: How to have a $5,000 trip to Chicago on a $500 budget

Find a cheap flight
Using the strategy we outlined you can snag a ticket to Chicago from Europe from $180 return. Potential saving $1,000.

Five star hotels and day passes
Last minute 5 star hotels deals. Check on the same day of your stay for cheap five star hotel deals. Go to enter Chicago, tonight, only one night an 5 stars. In low season this can be very effective on the weekends when hotels empty of their business travellers. Potential saving $800.

Restaurant deals
Nearly every restaurant in Chicago offers a midday menu for lunch at around $4 If you're on a budget, but like eating out, consider doing your dining in the daytime. You can also pick up street food everywhere for less than $1, just follow the locals - if they are queuing for a particular street cart's food, you can be sure its tasty. Potential saving $50.

Prioritise free entertainment
The average traveller spends $80 per DAY on entertainment in Chicago, but there's an abundance of free or cheap attractions that are just as amazing - expect the Grand Palace. That is absolutely worth your money. Potential saving $80.

Transport

Invest in a Chicago Transit Authority (CTA) pass for un-limited rides on buses and trains during your stay. Utilize free or low-cost trolley and shuttle services in the city.

The secret to saving HUGE amounts of money when traveling to Chicago...

is your mindset. Money is an emotional topic. If you associate words like "cheapskate" with saving money on things you don't care about while traveling, you are likely to say "F-it" and spend your money needlessly because you associate pain with saving money.

The good news is experiencing luxurious travel on a budget, tricks your brain into thinking you're already a high-roller, and you'll be more likely to act like one and invest your money.

While you still might think more money is the secret to saving huge amounts of money, the MANY lottery winners who have gone broke show us otherwise. For example, Andrew "Jack" Whittaker Jr. won a $315 million Powerball jackpot in 2002, which at the time was the largest lottery jackpot in history. He was robbed several times, lost millions of dollars gambling, and faced numerous legal problems, and had to grieve the drug-related death of his daughter.

I don't tell you this story to depress you before you visit Chicago, but to drive home the point that more money doesn't necessarily equal more luxury. If you are intentional with the money you spend, you can experience the greatest luxuries Chicago has to offer.

Saving money does not make you a cheapskate; it makes you smart. How do people get rich? They invest their money. They don't go out and earn it; they let their money earn more money. So every time you want to spend money, imagine this: while you travel, your money is working for you, not you for money. While you sleep, the money you've invested is growing. That's a pleasure a pricey entrance fee to an exhibition you don't want to see can't give you.

Thinking about putting your money to work for you tricks your brain into believing you are not withholding pleasure from yourself, you are saving your money to invest so you can go to even more amazing luxurious destinations. You are turning thrifty travel into a pleasure-fueled sport.

When you've got money invested, if you want to splash your cash on a first-class airplane seat, you can. I can't tell you how to invest your money, only that you should.

Travel, as the saying goes, is the only thing you spend money on that makes you richer. You can easily waste money, making it difficult to enjoy that metaphysical wealth. The biggest money-saving secret is to turn bargain hunting into a pleasurable activity, not an annoyance.

Budgeting consciously can be fun. Don't feel disappointed because you don't spend $150 to go into an overcrowded attraction. Feel good because soon that $150 will earn money for you. Meaning, you'll have the time and money to enjoy more metaphysical wealth while your bank balance increases.

So there it is. You can save a small fortune by being strategic with your trip planning. We've arranged everything in the guide to offer the best bang for your buck. Which means we took the view that if it's not an excellent investment for your money, we wouldn't include it. Why would a guide called 'Super Cheap' include lots of overpriced attractions? That said, if you think we've missed something or have unanswered questions, ping me an email: philgtang@gmail.com I'm on central Europe time and usually reply within 8 hours of getting your mail. We like to think of our guide books as evolving organisms helping our readers travel better cheaper. We use reader questions via email to update this book year round so you'll be helping other readers and yourself.

Don't put your dreams off!

Time is a currency you never get back and travel is its greatest return on investment. Plus, now you know you can visit Chicago for a fraction of the price most would have you believe.

Thank you for reading

Dear **Lovely Reader**,

If you have found this book useful, please consider writing a quick review on Amazon.

One person from every 1000 readers leaves a review on Amazon. It would mean more than you could ever know if you were one of our 1 in 1000 people to take the time to write a brief review.

We are a group of friends who all met traveling 15 years ago. We believe great experiences don't need to blow your budget, just your mind.

Thank you so much for reading again and for spending your time and investing your trips future in Super Cheap Insider Guides. One last note, please don't listen to anyone who says 'Oh no, you can't visit Chicago on a budget'. Unlike you, they didn't have this book. You can do ANYWHERE on a budget with the right insider advice and planning. Sure, learning to travel to Chicago on a budget that doesn't compromise on anything or drastically compromise on safety or comfort levels is a skill, but this guide has done the detective work for you. Now it is time for you to put the advice into action.

Phil and the Super Cheap Insider Guides Team

P.S If you need any more super cheap tips we'd love to hear from you e-mail me at philgtang@gmail.com, we have a lot of contacts in every region, so if there's a specific bargain you're hunting we can help you find it.

DISCOVER YOUR NEXT VACATION

☑ **LUXURY ON A BUDGET APPROACH**
☑ **CHOOSE FROM 107 DESTINATIONS**
☑ **EACH BOOK PACKED WITH REAL-TIME LOCAL TIPS**

All are available in Paperback and e-book on Amazon: https://www.amazon.com/dp/B09C2DHQG5

Several are available as audiobooks. You can watch excerpts of ALL for FREE on YouTube: https://youtube.com/channel/UCxo9YV8-M9P1cFosU-Gjnqg

Common pitfalls when it comes to al-locating money to your desires while traveling

Know your triggers

Studies have shown that people tend to spend more reck-lessly on vacation due to several factors, including psycho-logical, emotional, and environmental influences.

One study conducted by the American Psychological Asso-ciation found that people tend to overspend on vacation be-cause they view it as a time to indulge and reward them-selves for their hard work throughout the year. The study also found that vacationers tend to feel a sense of freedom and detachment from their daily routines, which can lead to impulsive spending behavior (APA, 2013).

Another study conducted by the University of Cambridge found that people tend to spend more on vacation because they are in a heightened emotional state, which can lead to a lack of impulse control. The study also found that the en-vironment in which people vacation can play a significant role in their spending behavior, as people tend to spend more when they are in a new and unfamiliar place (Prelec & Loewenstein, 1998).

A study published in the Journal of Consumer Psychology in 2015 found that people are more likely to indulge in hedonic (pleasure-seeking) purchases in the summer months. This is because people tend to be in a more positive mood during the summer, which leads to more impulsive spending.

Understanding these influences and setting a budget for a luxurious trip beforehand can help you make the most out of your vacation.

Beware of Malleable mental accounting

Let's say you budgeted spending only $30 per day in Chicago but then you say well if I was at home I'd be spending $30 on food as an everyday purchase so you add another $30 to your budget. Don't fall into that trap as the likelihood is you still have expenses at home even if its just the cost of keeping your freezer going.

Beware of impulse purchases in Chicago

Restaurants that you haven't researched and just idle into can sometimes turn out to be great, but more often, they turn out to suck, especially if they are near tourist attractions. Make yourself a travel itinerary including where you'll eat breakfast and lunch. Dinner is always more expensive, so the meal best to enjoy at home or as a takeaway. This book is full of incredible delicious eats. All you have to do is plan to go to them.

Social media and FOMO (Fear of Missing Out)

'The pull of seeing acquaintances spend money on travel can often be a more powerful motivator to spend more while traveling than seeing an advertisement.' Beware of what you allow to influence you and go back to the question, what's the best money I can spend today?

Now-or-never sales strategies

One reason tourists are targeted by salespeople is the success of the now-or-never strategy. If you don't spend the money now… your never get the opportunity again. Rarely is this true.

Instead of spending your money on something you might not actually desire, take five minutes. Ask yourself, do I really want this? And return to the answer in five minutes. Your body will either say an absolute yes with a warm, excited feeling or a no with a weak, obscure feeling.

Unexpected costs

"Holding on to anger is like grasping a hot coal with the intent of throwing it at someone else; you only hurt yourself." The Buddha.

One downside to traveling is unexpected costs. When these spring up from airlines, accommodation providers, tours and on and on, they feel like a punch in the gut. During the pandemic my earnings fell to 20% of what they are normally. No one was traveling, no one was buying travel guides. My accountant out of nowhere significantly raised his fee for the year despite the fact there was a lot less money to count. I was so angry I consulted a lawyer who told me you will spend more taking him to court than you will paying his bill. I had to get myself into a good feeling place before I paid his bill, so I googled how to feel good paying someone who has scammed you.

The answer: Write down that you will receive 10 times the amount you are paying from an unexpected source. I did that. Four months later, the accountant wrote to me. He had applied for a COVID subsidy for me and I would receive… you guessed it almost exactly 10 times his fee.

Make of that what you want. I don't wish to get embroiled in a conversation about what many term 'woo-woo', but the result of my writing that I would receive 10 times the amount made me feel much, much better when paying him. And ultimately, that was a gift in itself. So next time some airline or train operator or hotel/ Airbnb sticks you with an unexpected fee, immediately write that you will receive 10 times the amount you are paying from an unexpected source. Rise your vibe and skip the added price of feeling angry.

Hack your allocations for your Chicago Trip

"The best trick for saving is to eliminate the decision to save." Perry Wright of Duke University.

Put the money you plan to spend in Chicago on a pre-paid card in the local currency. This cuts out two problems - not knowing how much you've spent and totally avoiding expensive currency conversion fees.

You could even create separate spaces. This much for transportation, this for tours/entertainment, accommodation and food. We are reluctant to spend money that is pre-assigned to categories or uses.

Write that you want to enjoy a $3,000 trip for $500 to your Chicago trip. Countless research shows when you put goals in writing, you have a higher chance of following through.

Spend all the money you want to on buying experiences in Chicago

"Experiences are like good relatives that stay for a while and then leave. Objects are like relatives who move in and stay past their welcome." Daniel Gilbert, psychologist from Harvard University.

Economic and psychological research shows we are happier buying brief experiences on vacation rather than buying stuff to wear so give yourself freedom to spend on experiences knowing that the value you get back is many many times over.

Make saving money a game

There's one day a year where all the thrift shops where me and my family live sell everything there for a $1. My wife and I hold a contest where we take $5 and buy an entire outfit for each other. Whoever's outfit is liked more wins. We also look online to see whose outfit would have cost more to buy new. This year, my wife even snagged me an Armani coat for $1. I liked the coat when she showed it to me, but when I found out it was $500 new; I liked it and wore it a lot more.

Quadruple your money

Every-time you want to spend money, imagine it quadrupled. So the $10 you want to spend is actually $40. Now imagine that what you want to buy is four times the price. Do you still want it? If yes, go enjoy. If not, you've just saved yourself money, know you can choose to invest it in a way that quadruples or allocate it to something you really want to give you a greater return.

Understand what having unlimited amounts of money to spend in Chicago actually looks like

Let's look at what it would be like to have unlimited amounts of money to spend on your trip to Chicago.

Isolation

You take a private jet to your private Chicago hotel. There you are lavished with the best food, drink, and entertainment. Spending vast amounts of money on vacation equals being isolated.

If you're on your honeymoon and you want to be alone with your Amore, this is wonderful, but it can be equally wonderful to make new friends. Know this a study 'carried out by Brigham Young University, Utah found that while obesity increased risk of death by 30%, loneliness increased it by half.'

Comfort

Money can buy you late check outs of five-star hotels and priority boarding on airlines, all of which add up to comfort. But as this book has shown you, saving money in Chicago doesn't minimize comfort, that's just a lie travel agencies littered with glossy brochures want you to believe.

You can do late-check outs for free with the right credit cards and priority boarding can be purchased with a lot of airlines from $4. If you want to go big with first-class or business, flights offset your own travel costs by renting your own home or you can upgrade at the airport often for a fraction of what you would have paid booking a business flight online.

Best Discount websites for Luxury Travel

There are several discount websites that cater to luxury travelers and offer deals on high-end hotels, resorts, and other luxury travel experiences. Here are some of the best discount websites for luxury travel:

1. Secret Escapes: Secret Escapes offers exclusive deals on luxury hotels and vacations, with discounts of up to 60% off regular rates. Members receive email notifications about new deals, and can browse and book trips on the company's website or app.
2. Luxury Escapes: Luxury Escapes offers discounted rates on luxury hotels, resorts, and vacation packages around the world. M
3. Jetsetter: Jetsetter offers deals on luxury hotels and resorts, as well as curated travel experiences like private tours and cultural excursions.
4. Tablet Hotels: Tablet Hotels offers discounted rates on a curated selection of luxury hotels around the world, with a focus on design and boutique properties.
5. Vacationist: Vacationist offers members-only deals on luxury hotels, resorts, and vacation packages around the world.

MORE TIPS TO FIND CHEAP FLIGHTS

"The use of travelling is to regulate imagination by reality, and instead of thinking how things may be, to see them as they are." Samuel Jackson

If you're working full-time, you can save yourself a lot of money by requesting your time off from work starting in the middle of the week. Tuesdays and Wednesdays are the cheapest days to fly. You can save thousands just by adjusting your time off.

The simplest secret to booking cheap flights is open parameters. Let's say you want to fly from Chicago to Paris. You enter the USA in from and select France under to. You may find flights from New York City to Paris for $70. Then you just need to find a cheap flight to NYC. Make sure you calculate full costs, including if you need airport accommodation and of course getting to and from airports, **but in nearly every instance open parameters will save you at least half the cost of the flight.**

If you're not sure about where you want to go, use open parameters to show you the cheapest destinations from your city. Start with skyscanner.net they include the low-cost airlines that others like Kayak leave out. Google Flights can also show you cheap destinations. To see these leave the WHERE TO section blank.

Open parameters can also show you the cheapest dates to fly. If you're flexible, you can save up to 80% of the flight cost. Always check the weather at your destination before you book. Sometimes a $400 flight will be $20, because it's monsoon season. But hey, if you like the rain, why not?

ALWAYS USE A PRIVATE BROWSER TO BOOK FLIGHTS

Skyscanner and other sites track your IP address and put prices up and down based on what they determine your strength of conviction to buy. e.g. if you've booked one-way and are looking for the return, these sites will jack the prices up by in most cases 50%. Incognito browsing pays.

Use a VPN such as Hola to book your flight from your destination

Install Hola, change your destination to the country you are flying to. The location from which a ticket is booked can affect the price significantly as algorithms consider local buying power.

Choose the right time to buy your ticket.

Choose the right time to buy your ticket, as purchasing tickets on a Sunday has been proven to be cheaper. If you can only book during the week, try to do it on a Tuesday.

Mistake fares

Email alerts from individual carriers are where you can find the best 'mistake fares". This is where a computer error has resulted in an airline offering the wrong fare. In my experience, it's best to sign up to individual carriers email lists, but if you ARE lazy Secret Flying puts together a daily roster of mistake fares. Visit https://www.secretflying.com/errorfare/ to see if there're any errors that can benefit you.

Fly late for cheaper prices

Red-eye flights, the ones that leave later in the day, are typically cheaper and less crowded, so aim to book that flight if possible. You will also get through the airport much quicker at the end of the day. Just make sure there's ground transport available for when you land. You don't want to save $50 on the airfare and spend it on a taxi to your accommodation.

Use this APP for same day flights

If your plans are flexible, use 'Get The Flight Out' (http://www.gtfoflights.com/) a fare tracker Hopper that shows you same-day deeply discounted flights. This is best for long-haul flights with major carriers. You can often find a British Airways round-trip from JFK Airport to Heathrow for $300. If you booked this in advance, you'd pay at least double.

Take an empty water bottle with you

Airport prices on food and drinks are sky high. It disgusts me to see some airports charging $10 for a bottle of water. ALWAYS take an empty water bottle with you. It's relatively unknown, but most airports have drinking water fountains past the security check. Just type in your airport name to wateratairports.com to locate the fountain. Then once you've passed security (because they don't allow you to take 100ml or more of liquids) you can freely refill your bottle with water.

Round-the-World (RTW) Tickets

It is always cheaper to book your flights using a DIY approach. First, you may decide you want to stay longer in one country, and a RTW will charge you a hefty fee for changing your flight. Secondly, it all depends on where and when you travel and as we have discussed, there are many ways to ensure you pay way less than $1,500 for a year of flights. If you're travelling long-haul, the best strategy is to buy a return ticket, say New York, to Bangkok and then take cheap flights or transport around Asia and even to Australia and beyond.

Cut your costs to and from airports

Don't you hate it when getting to and from the airport is more expensive than your flight! And this is true in so many cities, especially European ones. For some reason, Google often shows the most expensive options. Use Omio to compare the cheapest transport options and save on airport transfer costs.

Car sharing instead of taxis

Check if Chicago has car sharing at the airport. Often they'll be tons of cars parked at the airport that are half the price of taking a taxi into the city. In most instances, you register your driving licence on an app and scan the code on the car to get going.

Checking Bags

Sometimes you need to check bags. If you do, put an AirTag inside. That way, you'll be about to see when you land where your bag is. This saves you the nail biting wait at baggage claim. And if worse comes to worst, and you see your bag is actually in another city, you can calmly stroll over to customer services and show them where your bag is.

Is it cheaper and more convenient to send your bags ahead?

Before you check your bags, check if it's cheaper to send them ahead of you with sendmybag.com obviously if you're staying in an Airbnb, you'll need to ask the hosts permission or you can time them to arrive the day after you. Hotels are normally very amenable.

What Credit Card Gives The Best Air Miles?

You can slash the cost of flights just for spending on a piece of plastic.

LET'S TALK ABOUT DEBT

Before we go into the best cards for each country, let's first talk about debt. The US system offers the best and biggest rewards. Why? Because they rely on the fact that many people living in the US will not pay their cards in full and the card will earn the bank significant interest payments. Other countries have a very different attitude towards money, debt, and saving than Americans. Thus in Germany and Austria the offerings aren't as favourable as the UK, Spain and Australia, where debt culture is more widely embraced. The takeaway here is this: **Only spend on one of these cards when you have set-up an automatic total monthly balance repayment. Don't let banks profit from your lizard brain!**

For those in the USA with bad credit

It's important to note that credit card companies generally reserve the most generous rewards and perks for customers with good or excellent credit scores. However, some credit cards may still offer miles or rewards for those with bad credit scores, but the benefits and rewards may be more limited.

One example of a credit card that may offer rewards for those with bad credit scores is the Milestone Gold Mastercard. This card offers 1% cash back on every purchase and has no annual fee, making it a good option for those looking to earn rewards while building credit.

Another option is the Capital One QuicksilverOne Cash Rewards Credit Card. This card offers 1.5% cash back on all purchases and has a higher annual fee than the Milestone Gold Mastercard, but it may still be a good option for those with bad credit scores who are looking to earn rewards.

The best air-mile credit cards for those living in the UK

Amex Preferred Rewards Gold comes out top for those living in the UK for 2023.

Here are the benefits:

- 20,000-point bonus on £3,000 spend in first three months. These can be used towards flights with British Airways, Virgin Atlantic, Emirates and Etihad, and often other rewards, such as hotel stays and car hire.
- 1 point per £1 spent
- 1 point = 1 airline point
- Two free visits a year to airport lounges
- No fee in year one, then £140/yr

The downside:

- Fail to repay fully and it's 59.9% rep APR interest, incl fee

You'll need to cancel before the £140/yr fee kicks in year two if you want to avoid it.

The best air-mile credit cards for those living in Canada

Aeroplan is the superior rewards program in Canada. The card has a high earn rate for Aeroplan Points, generating 1.5 points per $1 spent on eligible purchases. Look at the specifics of the eligible purchases https://www.aircanada.com/ca/en/aco/home/aeroplan/earn.html. If you're not spending on these things AMEX's Membership Rewards program offers you the best returns in Canada.

The best air-mile credit cards for those living in Germany

If you have a German bank account, you can apply for a Lufthansa credit card.

Earn 50,000 award miles if you spend $3,000 in purchases and paying the annual fee, both within the first 90 days.

Earn 2 award miles per $1 spent on ticket purchases directly from Miles & More integrated airline partners.

Earn 1 award mile per $1 spent on all other purchases.

The downsides

the €89 annual fee

Limited to fly with Lufthansa and its partners but you can capitalise on perks like the companion pass and airport lounge vouchers.

You need excellent credit to get this card.

The best air-mile credit cards for those living in Austria

"In Austria, Miles & More offers you a special credit card. You get miles for each purchase with the credit card. The Miles & More program calculates miles earned based on the distance flown and booking class. For European flights, the booking class is a flat rate. For intercontinental flights, mileage is calculated by multiplying the booking class by the distance flown." They offer a calculator so you can see how many points you could earn: https://www.miles-and-more.com/at/en/earn/airlines/mileage-calculator.html

The best air-mile credit cards for those living in Spain:

"The American Express card is the best known and oldest to earn miles, thanks to its membership Rewards program. When making payments with this card, points are added, which can then be exchanged for miles from airlines such as Iberia, Air Europa, Emirates or Alitalia." More information is available here: https://www.americanexpress.com/es-es/

The best air-mile credit cards for those living in Australia

ANZ Rewards Black comes out top for 2023.

180,000 bonus ANZ Reward Points (can get an $800 gift card) and $0 annual fee for the first year with the ANZ Rewards Black
Points Per Spend: 1 Velocity point on purchases of up to $5,000 per statement period and 0.5 Velocity points thereafter.
Annual Fee: $0 in the first year, then $375 after.
Ns no set minimum income required, however, there is a minimum credit limit of $15,000 on this card.

Here are some ways you can hack points onto this card: https://www.pointhacks.com.au/credit-cards/anz-rewards-black-guide/

The best air-mile credit card solution for those living in the USA with a POOR credit score

The downside to Airline Mile cards is that they require good or excellent credit scores, meaning 690 or higher.

If you have bad credit and want to use credit card air lines you will need to rebuild your credit poor. The Credit One Bank® Platinum Visa® for Rebuilding Credit is a good credit card for people with bad credit who don't want to place a deposit on a secured card. The Credit One Platinum Visa offers a $300 credit limit, rewards, and the potential for credit-limit increases, which in time will help rebuild your score.

PLEASE don't sign-up for any of these cards if you can't trust yourself to repay it in full monthly. This will only lead to stress for you.

Frequent Flyer Memberships

"Points" and "miles" are often used interchangeably, but they're usually two very different things. Maximise and diversify your rewards by utilising both.

A frequent-flyer program (FFP) is a loyalty program offered by an airline. They are designed to encourage airline customers to fly more to accumulate points (also called miles, kilometres, or segments) which can be redeemed for air travel or other rewards.

You can sign up with any FFP program for free. There are three major airline alliances in the world: Oneworld, SkyTeam and Star Alliance. I am with One World https://www.oneworld.com/members because the points can be accrued and used for most flights.

The best return on your points is to use them for international business or first class flights with lie-flat seats. You would need 3 times more miles compared to an economy flight, but if you paid cash, you'd pay 5 - 10 times more than the cost of the economy flight, so it really pays to use your points only for upgrades. The worst value for your miles is to buy an economy seat or worse, a gift from the airlines gift-shop.

Sign up for a family/household account to pool miles together. If you share a common address, you can claim the miles with most airlines. You can use AwardWallet to keep track of your miles. Remember that they only last for 2 years, so use them before they expire.

How to get 70% off a Cruise

An average cruise can set you back $4,000. If you dream of cruising the oceans, but find the pricing too high, look at repositioning cruises. You can save as much as 70% by taking a cruise which takes the boat back to its home port.

These one-way itineraries take place during low cruise seasons when ships have to reposition themselves to locations where there's warmer weather.

To find a repositioning cruise, go to vacationstogo.com/repositioning_cruises.cfm. This simple and often over-looked booking trick is great for avoiding long flights with children and can save you so much money!

It's worth noting we don't have any affiliations with any travel service or provider. The links we suggest are chosen based on our experience of finding the best deals.

Hotel Loyalty Programs

There are several hotel loyalty programs that offer rewards and benefits for frequent travelers. Here are some of the best:

1. Marriott Bonvoy: Marriott Bonvoy is one of the largest hotel loyalty programs, with over 30 hotel brands and over 7,000 properties around the world. Members can earn points for their stays and redeem them for free nights, upgrades, and other benefits. Marriott Bonvoy offers elite status levels with perks like lounge access, late checkout, and free breakfast.
2. Hilton Honors: Hilton Honors is another popular hotel loyalty program with over 6,000 properties worldwide. Members can earn points for their stays and redeem them for free nights, room upgrades, and other benefits. Hilton Honors offers elite status levels with perks like lounge access, late checkout, and free breakfast.
3. World of Hyatt: World of Hyatt is a loyalty program that offers rewards and benefits for stays at Hyatt properties around the world. Members can earn points for their stays and redeem them for free nights, room upgrades, and other benefits. World of Hyatt offers elite status levels with perks like lounge access, late checkout, and free breakfast.
4. IHG Rewards Club: IHG Rewards Club is a loyalty program that includes several hotel brands, including InterContinental, Crowne Plaza, and Holiday Inn. Members can earn points for their stays and redeem them for free nights, room upgrades, and other benefits. IHG Rewards Club offers elite status levels with perks like lounge access, late checkout, and free breakfast.

5. Accor Live Limitless: Accor Live Limitless is a loyalty program that includes several hotel brands, including Sofitel, Pullman, and Novotel. Members can earn points for their stays and redeem them for free nights, room upgrades, and other benefits. Accor Live Limitless offers elite status levels with perks like lounge access, late checkout, and free breakfast.

These hotel loyalty programs can offer valuable rewards and benefits for frequent travelers. The best program for you will depend on your travel preferences and the hotel brands you prefer to stay with. It's worth considering which program offers the most valuable rewards for your travel patterns and selecting a program that fits your needs.

Pack like a Pro

"He who would travel happily must travel light." – Antoine de St. Exupery 59.

Travel as lightly as you can. We always need less than we think. You will be very grateful that you have a light pack when changing trains, travelling through the airport, catching a bus, walking to your accommodation, or climbing stairs.

Make a list of what you will wear for 7 days and take only those clothes. You can easily wash your things while you're travelling if you stay in an Airbnb with a washing machine or visit a local laundrette. Roll your clothes for maximum space usage and fewer wrinkles. If you feel really nervous about travelling with such few things, make sure you have a dressier outfit, a little black dress for women is always valuable, a shirt for men. Then pack shorts, a long pair of pants, loose tops and a hoodie to snuggle in. Remind yourself that a lack of clothing options is an opportunity to find bargain new outfits in thrift stores. You can either sell these on eBay after you've worn them or post them home to yourself. You'll feel less stressed, as you don't have to look after or feel weighed down by excess baggage. Here are three things to remember when packing:

- Co-ordinate colours - make sure everything you bring can be worn together.

- Be happy to do laundry - fresh clothes when you're travelling feels very luxurious.

- Take liquid minis no bigger than 60ml. Liquid is heavy, and you simply don't need to carry so much at one time.

- Buy reversible clothes (coats are a great idea), dresses which can be worn multiple different ways.

Checks to Avoid Fees

Always have 6 months' validity on your passport

To enter most countries, you need 6 months from the day you land. Factor in different time zones around the world if your passport is on the edge. Airport security will stop you from boarding your flight at the airport if your passport has 5 months and 29 days left.

Google Your Flight Number before you leave for the airport

Easily find out where your plane is from anywhere. Confirm the status of your flight before you leave for the airport with flightaware.com. This can save you long unnecessary wait times.

Check-in online

The founder, Ryan O'Leary of budget airline Ryanair famously said: "We think they should pay €60 for [failing to check-in online] being so stupid.". Always check-in online, even for international flights. Cheaper international carriers like Scoot will charge you at the airport to check-in.

Checking Bags

Never, ever check a bag if you can avoid it. Sometimes you need to check bags. If you do, put an AirTag inside. That way, you'll be about to see when you land where your bag is. This saves you the nail biting wait at baggage claim. And if worse comes to worst, and you see your bag is actually in another city, you can calmly stroll over to customer services and show them where your bag is.

Is it cheaper and more convenient to send your bags ahead?

Before you check your bags, check if it's cheaper to send them ahead of you with sendmybag.com obviously if you're staying in an Airbnb, you'll need to ask the hosts permission or you can time them to arrive the day after you. Hotels are normally very amenable.

It is always cheaper to put heavier items on a ship, rather than take them on a flight with you. Find the best prices for shipping at https://www.parcelmonkey.com/delivery-services/shipping-heavy-items

Use a fragile sticker

Put a 'Fragile' sticker on anything you check to ensure that it's handled better as it goes through security. It'll also be one of the first bags released after the flight, getting you out of the airport quicker.

If you check your bag, photograph it

Take a photo of your bag before you check it. This will speed up the paperwork if it is damaged or lost.

Airport Lounges

The best way to relax at the airport is in a lounge where they provide free food, drinks, comfortable chairs, luxurious amenities (many have showers) and, if you're lucky, a peaceful ambience. If you're there for a longer time, look for Airport Cubicles, sleep pods which charge by the hour.

You can use your FFP Card (Frequent Flyer Memberships) to get into select lounges for free. Check your eligibility before you pay.

If you're travelling a lot, I'd recommend investing in a Priority Pass for the airport.

It includes 850-plus airport lounges around the world. The cost is $99 for the year and $27 per lounge visit or you can pay $399 for the year all inclusive.

If you need a lounge for a one-off day, you can get a Day Pass. Buy it online for a discount, it always works out cheaper than buying at the airport. Use www.LoungePass.com.

Lounges are also great if you're travelling with kids, as they're normally free for kids and will definitely cost you less than snacks for your little ones. The rule is that kids should be seen and not heard, so consider this before taking an overly excited child who wants to run around, or you might be asked to leave even after you've paid.

How to spend money

Bank ATM fees vary from $2.50 per transaction to as high as $5 or more, depending on the ATM and the country. You can completely skip those fees by paying with card and using a card which can hold multiple currencies.

Budget travel hacking begins with a strategy to spend without fees. Your individual strategy depends on the country you legally reside in as to what cards are available. Happily there are some fin-tech solutions which can save you thousands on those pesky ATM withdrawal fees and are widely available globally. Here are a selection of cards you can pre-charge with currency for Chicago:

N26

N26 is a 12-year-old digital bank. I have been using them for over 6 years. The key advantage is fee-free card transactions abroad. They have a very elegant app, where you can check your timeline for all transactions listed in real time or manage your in-app security anywhere. The card you receive is a Mastercard so you can use it everywhere. If you lose the card, you don't have to call anyone, just open the app and swipe 'lock card'. It puts your purchases into a graph automatically so you can see what you spend on. You can open an account from abroad entirely online, all you need is your passport and a camera n26.com

Revolut

Revolut is a multi-currency account that allows you to hold and exchange 29 currencies and spend fee-free abroad. It's a UK based neobank, but accepts customers from all over the world.

Wise debit card

If you're going to be in one place for a long time, the Wise debit card is like having your travel money on a card – it lets you spend money at the real exchange rate.

Monzo

Monzo is good if your UK based. They offer a fee-free UK account. Fee-free international money transfers and fee-free spending abroad.

The downside

The cards above are debit cards, meaning you need to have money in those accounts to spend it. This comes with one big downside: safety. Credit card issuers' have "zero liability" meaning you're not liable for unauthorised charges. All the cards listed above do provide cover for unauthorised charges but times vary greatly in how quickly you'd get your money back if it were stolen.

The best option is to check in your country to see which credit cards are the best for travelling and set up monthly payments to repay the whole amount so you don't pay un-necessary interest. In the USA, Schwab regularly ranks at the top for travel credit cards. Credit cards are always the safer option when abroad simply because you get your money back faster if its stolen and if you're renting cars, most will give you free insurance when you book the car rental using the card, saving you money.

Always withdraw money; never exchange.

Money exchanges, whether they be on the streets or in the airports will NEVER give you a good exchange rate. Do not bring bundles of cash. Instead, withdraw local currency from the ATM as needed and try to use only free ATMs. Many in airports charge you a fee to withdraw cash. Look for bigger ATMs attached to banks to avoid this.

Recap

- Take cash from local, non-charging ATMs for the best rates.

- Never change at airport exchange desks unless you absolutely have to, then just change just enough to be able get to a bank ATM.

- Bring a spare credit card for emergencies.

- Split cash in various places on your person (pock-ets, shoes) and in your luggage. It's never sensible to keep your cash or cards all in one place.

- In higher risk areas, use a money belt under your clothes or put $50 in your shoe or bra.

How NOT to be ripped off

"One of the great things about travel is that you find out ho
w many good, kind people there are."
— Edith Wharton

The quote above may seem ill placed in a chapter entitled
how not to be ripped off, but I included it to remind you
that the vast majority of people do not want to rip you off.
In fact, scammers are normally limited to three situations:

1. Around heavily visited attractions - these places are
   targeted purposively due to sheer footfall. Many
   criminals believe ripping people off is simply a num-
   bers game.

2. In cities or countries with low-salaries or communist
   ideologies. If they can't make money in the country,
   they seek to scam foreigners. If you have travelled to
   India, Morocco or Cuba you will have observed this
   phenomenon.

3. When you are stuck and the person helping you
   know you have limited options.

Scammers know that most people will avoid confrontation.
Don't feel bad about utterly ignoring someone and saying
no. Here are six strategies to avoid being ripped off:

1. **Never ever agree to pay as much as you want.
   Always decide on a price before.**

Whoever you're dealing with is trained to tell you, they are
uninterested in money. This is a trap. If you let people do

this they will ask for MUCH MORE money at the end, and because you have used there service, you will feel obliged to pay. This is a conman's trick and nothing more.

2. Pack light

You can move faster and easier. If you take heavy luggage, you will end up taking taxis which are comparatively very costly over time.

3. NEVER use the airport taxi service. Book a private transfer or plan to use public transport before you reach the airport.

4. Don't buy a sim card from the airport. Buy from the local supermarkets it will cost 50% less.

5. Eat at local restaurants serving regional food

Food defines culture. Exploring all delights available to the palate doesn't need to cost enormous sums.

6. Ask the locals what something should cost, and try not to pay over that.

7. If you find yourself with limited options. e.g. your taxi dumps you on the side of the road because you refuse to pay more (common in India and parts of South America) don't act desperate and negotiate as if you have other options or you will be extorted.

8. Don't blindly rely on social media[4]

Let's say you post in a Facebook group that you want tips for travelling to The Maldives. A lot of the comments you will receive come from guides, hosts and restaurants doing

---

[4] https://arstechnica.com/tech-policy/2019/12/social-media-platforms-leave-95-of-reported-fake-accounts-up-study-finds/

their own promotion. It's estimated that 50% or more of Facebook's current monthly active users are fake. And what's worse, a recent study found Social media platforms leave 95% of reported fake accounts up. These accounts are the digital versions of the men who hang around the Grand Palace in Bangkok telling tourists its closed, to divert you to shops where they will receive a commission for bringing you.

It can also be the case that genuine comments come from people who have totally different interests, beliefs and yes, budgets to yours. Make your experience your own and don't believe every comment you read.

Bottom line: use caution when accepting recommendations on social media and always fact-check with your own research.

Small tweaks on the road add up to big differences in your bank balance

Take advantage of other hotel amenities

If you fancy a swim but you're nowhere near the ocean, try the nearest hotel with a pool. As long as you buy a drink, the hotel staff will probably grant you access.

Fill up your mini bar for free.

Fill up your mini bar for free by storing things from the breakfast bar or grocery shop in your mini bar to give you a greater selection of drinks and food without the hefty price tag.

Save yourself some ironing

Use the steam from the shower to get rid of wrinkles in clothing. If something is creased, leave it trapped with the steam in the bathroom overnight for even better results.

See somewhere else for free

Opt for long stopovers, allowing you to experience another city without spending much money.

Wear your heaviest clothes

On the plane to save weight in your pack, allowing you to bring more with you. Big coats can then be used as pillows to make your flight more comfortable.

Don't get lost while you're away.

Find where you want to go using Google Maps, then type 'OK Maps' into the search bar to store this information for offline viewing.

Use car renting services

Share Now or Car2Go allow you to hire a car for 2 hours for $25 in a lot of European countries.

Share Rides

Use sites like blablacar.com to find others who are driving in your direction. It can be 80% cheaper than normal transport. Just check the drivers reviews.

Use free gym passes

Get a free gym day pass by googling the name of a local gym and free day pass.

When asked by people providing you a service where you are from..

If there's no price list for the service you are asking for, when asked where you are from, Say you are from a lesser-known poorer country. I normally say Macedonia, and if they don't know where it is, add it's a poor country. If you say UK, USA, the majority of Europe bar the well-known poorer countries taxi drivers, tour operators etc will match the price to what they think you pay at home.

Set-up a New Uber/ other car hailing app account for discounts

By googling you can find offers with $50 free for new users in most cities for Uber/ Lyft/ Bolt and alike. Just set up a new gmail.com email account to take advantage.

Where and How to Make Friends

"People don't take trips, trips take people." – John Stein-beck

Become popular at the airport

Want to become popular at the airport? Pack a power bar with multiple outlets and just see how many friends you can make. It's amazing how many people forget their chargers, or who packed them in the luggage that they checked in.

Stay in Hostels

First of all, Hostels don't have to be shared dorms, and they cater to a much wider demographic than is assumed. Hostels are a better environment for meeting people than hotels, and more importantly they tended to open up excursion opportunities that further opened up that opportunity.

Or take up a hobby

If hostels are a definite no-no for you; find an interest. Take up a hobby where you will meet people. I've dived for years and the nature of diving is you're always paired up with a dive buddy. I met a lot of interesting people that way.

When unpleasantries come your way...

We all have our good and bad days travelling, and on a bad day you can feel like just taking a flight home. Here are some ways to overcome common travel problems:

Anxiety when flying

It has been over 40 years since a plane has been brought down by turbulence. Repeat that number to yourself: 40 years! Planes are built to withstand lighting strikes, extreme storms and ultimately can adjust course to get out of their way. Landing and take-off are when the most accidents happen, but you have statistically three times the chance of winning a huge jackpot lottery, then you do of dying in a plane crash.

If you feel afraid on the flight, focus on your breathing saying the word 'smooth' over and over until the flight is smooth. Always check the airline safety record on airliner-ating.com I was surprised to learn Ryanair and Easyjet as much less safe than Wizz Air according to those ratings because they sell similarly priced flights. If there is extreme turbulence, I feel much better knowing I'm in a 7 star safety plane.

Wanting to sleep instead of seeing new places

This is a common problem. Just relax, there's little point doing fun things when you feel tired. Factor in jet-lag to your travel plans. When you're rested and alert you'll enjoy your new temporary home much more. Many people hate the first week of a long-trip because of jet-lag and often blame this on their first destination, but its rarely true. Ask

209 of 227

travellers who 'hate' a particular place and you will see that very often they either had jet-lag or an unpleasant journey there.

Going over budget

Come back from a trip to a monster credit card bill? Hopefully, this guide has prevented you from returning to an unwanted bill. Of course, there are costs that can creep up and this is a reminder about how to prevent them making their way on to your credit card bill:

- To and from the airport. Solution: leave adequate time and take the cheapest method - book before.

- Baggage. Solution: take hand luggage and post things you might need to yourself.

- Eating out. Solution: go to cheap eats places and suggest those to friends.

- Parking. Solution: use apps to find free parking

- Tipping. Solution Leave a modest tip and tell the server you will write them a nice review.

- Souvenirs. Solution: fridge magnets only.

- Giving to the poor. (This one still gets me, but if you're giving away $10 a day - it adds up) Solution: volunteer your time instead and recognise that in tourist destinations many beggars are run by organised crime gangs.

Price v Comfort

I love traveling. I don't love struggling. I like decent accommodation, being able to eat properly and see places and enjoy. I am never in the mood for low-cost airlines or crappy transfers, so here's what I do to save money.

- Avoid organised tours unless you are going to a place where safety is a real issue. They are expensive and constrain your wanderlust to typical things. I only recommend them in Algeria, Iran and Papua New Guinea - where language and gender views pose serious problems all cured by a reputable tour organiser.

- Eat what the locals do.

- Cook in your Airbnb/ hostel where restaurants are expensive.

- Shop at local markets.

- Spend time choosing your flight, and check the operator on arilineratings.com

Not knowing where free toilets are

Use Toilet Finder - https://play.google.com/store/apps/details?id=com.bto.toilet&hl=en

Your Airbnb is awful

Airbnb customer service is notoriously bad. Help yourself out. Try to sort things out with the host, but if you can't, take photos of everything e.g bed, bathroom, mess, doors, contact them within 24 hours. Tell them you had to leave and pay for new accommodation. Ask politely for a full refund including booking fees. With photographic evidence and your new accommodation receipt, they can't refuse.

The airline loses your bag

Go to the Luggage desk before leaving the airport and report the bag missing. Hopefully you've headed the advice to put an AirTag in your checked bag and you can show them where to find your bag. Most airlines will give you an overnight bag, ask where you're staying and return the bag to you within three days. It's extremely rare for Airlines to lose your bag due to technological innovation, but if that happens you should submit an insurance claim after the three days is up, including receipts for everything you had to buy in the interim.

Your travel companion lets you down

Whether it's a breakup or a friend cancelling, it sucks and can ramp up costs. The easiest solution to finding a new travel companion is to go to a well-reviewed hostel and find someone you want to travel with. You should spend at least three days getting to know this person before you suggest travelling together. Finding someone in person is always better than finding someone online, because you can get a better idea of whether you will have a smooth journey together. Travel can make or break friendships.

Culture shock

I had one of the strongest culture shocks while spending 6 months in Japan. It was overwhelming how much I had to prepare when I went outside of the door (googling words and sentences what to use, where to go, which station and train line to use, what is this food called in Japanese and how does its look etc.). I was so tired constantly but in the end I just let go and went with my extremely bad Japanese. If you feel culture shocked its because your brain is referencing your surroundings to what you know. Stop comparing, have Google translate downloaded and relax.

Your Car rental insurance is crazy expensive

I always use carrentals.com and book with a credit card. Most credit cards will give you free insurance for the car, so you don't need to pay the extra. Some unsavoury companies will bump the price up when you arrive. Ask to speak to a manager. If this doesn't resolve, it google "consumer ombudsman for NAME OF COUNTRY." and seek an immediate full refund on the balance difference you paid. It is illegal in most countries to alter the price of a rental car when the person arrives to pickup a pre-arranged car.

A note on Car Rental Insurance

Always always always rent a car with a credit card that has rental vehicle coverage built into the card and is automatically applied when you rent a car. Then there's no need to buy additional rental insurance (check with your card on the coverage they protect some exclude collision coverage). Do yourself a favour when you step up to the desk to rent the car tell the agent you're already covered and won't be buying anything today. They work on commission and you'll save time and your patience avoiding the upselling.

You're sick

First off ALWAYS, purchase travel insurance. Including emergency transport up to $500k even to back home, which is usually less than $10 additional. I use https://www.comparethemarket.com/travel-insurance/ to find the best days. If I am sick I normally check into a hotel with room service and ride it out.

Make a Medication Travel Kit

Take travel sized medications with you:

- Antidiarrheal medication (for example, bismuth sub-salicylate, loperamide)

- Medicine for pain or fever (such as acetaminophen, aspirin, or ibuprofen)

- Throat Lozenges

Save yourself from most travel related hassles

- Do not make jokes with immigration and customs staff. A misunderstanding can lead to HUGE fines.

- Book the most direct flight you can find nonstop if possible.

- Carry a US$50 bill for emergency cash. I have entered a country and all ATM and credit card systems were down. US$ can be exchanged nearly anywhere in the world and is useful in extreme situations, but where possible don't exchange, as you will lose money.

- Check, and recheck, required visas and such BEFORE the day of your trip. Some countries, for instance, require a ticket out of the country in order to enter. Others, like the US and Australia, require electronic authorisation in advance.

- Airport security is asinine and inconsistent around the world. Keep this in mind when connecting flights. Always leave at least 2 hours for international connections or international to domestic. In Stansted for example, they force you to buy one of their plastic bags, and remove your liquids from your own plastic bag.... just to make money from you. And this adds to the time it will take to get through security, so lines are long.

- Wiki travel is perfect to use for a lay of the land.

- Expensive luggage rarely lasts longer than cheap luggage, in my experience. Fancy leather bags are toast with air travel.

Food

- When it comes to food, eat in local restaurants, not tourist-geared joints. Any place with the menu in three or more languages is going to be overpriced.

- Take a spork - a knife, spoon and fork all in one.

Water Bottle

Take a water bottle with a filter. We love these ones from Water to Go.

Empty it before airport security and separate the bottle and filter as some airport people will try and claim it has liquids…

Bug Sprays

If you're heading somewhere tropical spray your clothes with Permethrin before you travel. It lasts 40 washes and saves space in your bag. A 'Bite Away' zapper can be used after the bite to totally erase it. It cuts down on the itching and erases the bite from your skin.

Order free mini's

Don't buy those expensive travel sized toiletries, order travel sized freebies online. This gives you the opportunity to try brands you've never used before, and who knows, you might even find your new favourite soap.

Take a waterproof bag

If you're travelling alone you can swim without worrying about your phone, wallet and passport laying on the beach. You can also use it as a source of entertainment on those ultra budget flights.

Make a private entertainment centre anywhere

Always take an eye-mask, earplugs, a scarf and a kindle reader - so you can sleep and entertain yourself anywhere!

The best Travel Gadgets

The door alarm

If you're nervous and staying in private rooms or airbnbs take a door alarm. For those times when you just don't feel safe, it can help you fall asleep. You can get tiny ones for less than $10.

Smart Blanket

Amazon sells a 6 in 1 heating blanket that is very useful for cold trips. Its great if you have poor circulation as it becomes a detachable Foot Warmer.

The coat that becomes a tent

https://www.adiff.com/products/tent-jacket. This is great if you're going to be doing a lot of camping.

Safety

"If you think adventure is dangerous, try routine. It's lethal." – Paulo Coelho

Traveller murdered is a media headline that leads people to think traveling is more dangerous than it is. The media sensationalise the rare murders and deaths of backpackers and travellers. The actual chances of you dying abroad are extremely extremely low.

There are many things you can to keep yourself safe. Here are our tips.

1. Always check fco.co.uk before travelling. NEVER RELY on websites or books. Things are changing constantly and the FCO's (UK's foreign office) advice is always UP TO DATE (hourly) and **extremely conservative**.

2. Check your mindset. I've travelled alone to over 180 countries and the main thing I learnt is if you walk around scared, or anticipating you're going to be pickpocketed, your constant fear will attract bad energy. Murders or attacks on travellers are the mainstay of media, not reality, especially in countries familiar with travellers. The only place I had cause to genuinely fear for my life was Papua New Guinea - where nothing actually happened to me only my own panic over culture shock.

There are many things you can do to stop yourself being victim to the two main problems when travelling: theft or being scammed.

Here are my top tips:

- Stay alert while you're out and always have an exit strategy.

- Keep your money in a few different places on your person and your passport somewhere it can't be grabbed.

- Take a photo of your passport on your phone in case. If you do lose it, google for your embassy, you can usually get a temporary pretty fast.

- Google safety tips for travelling in your country to help yourself out and memorise the emergency number.

- At hostels, keep your large bag in the room far under the bed/out of the way with a lock on the zipper.

- On buses/trains, I would even lock my bag to the luggage rack.

- Get a personal keychain alarm. The sound will scare anyone away.

- Don't turn your back to traffic while you use your phone.

- When travelling in a tuktuk sit in the middle and keep your bag secure. Wear sunglasses as dust can easily get in your eyes.

- Don't let anyone give you flowers, bracelets, or any type of trinket, even if they insist it's for free and compliment you like crazy.

- Don't let strangers know that you are alone - unless they are travel friends.

- Lastly, and most importantly -Trust your gut! If it doesn't feel right, it isn't.

How I got hooked on I Luxury Travel on a Budget

My dad loved walking up to the lobby desk of a five-star hotel without a care in the world. So much so that he booked overpriced holidays on credit cards, a lot of them. However, as it turned out, we couldn't afford any of them. In the end, my dad had no choice but to declare bankruptcy, and when my mum realized the extent of the debt he had accumulated, our family unit dissolved. This painful experience led me to my life's passion: luxury budget travel.

As someone who has experienced the suffocating burden of debt firsthand, I understand that being on vacation does not excuse reckless spending. In fact, it goes against the very idea of travel, which is supposed to bring freedom.

Before I began writing my Super Cheap Insider guides, many people told me that my dream of luxurious budget travel was impossible. However, I knew from personal experience that it could be done by using local insider hacks. I hope this guide proves to you that budget travel can indeed be luxurious.

A final word...

There's a simple system you can use to think about luxury budget travel. In life, we can choose two of the following: cheap, fast, or quality. So if you want it Cheap and fast you will get a lower quality service. Fast-food is the perfect example. The system holds true for purchasing anything while travelling. I always choose cheap and quality, except at times where I am really limited on time. Ultimately, you must make choices about what's most important to you and heed your heart's desires.

'Your heart is the most powerful muscle in your body. Do what it says.' Jen Sincero

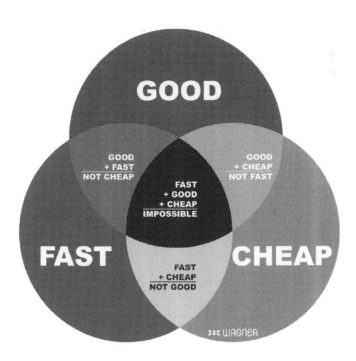

If you've found this book useful, please leave a quick review.

Your feedback is extremely valuable to me and will help others decide if this book is right for them. Thank you in advance for your support!

Copyright

Made in the USA
Middletown, DE
10 November 2024

64237834R00126